Bird Quest

Bird Quest

A Personal Odyssey

by

JAMES STEEL

Drawings by James Alder

Bridge Studios
Northumberland
1989

To Margaret, my late wife, who travelled with me on several of my expeditions. She took a keen interest in the preparation of this book, and was always an inspiration.

First published in Great Britain in 1989
by Bridge Studios and Sir James Steel
Kirklands
The Old Vicarage
Scremerston
Berwick upon Tweed
Northumberland TD15 2RB
Tel.: 0289 302658/330274

© James Steel 1989
Illustrations © James Alder 1989

ISBN 0 9512630 8 0

Jacket design by James Alder

Typeset by EMS Phototypesetting, Berwick upon Tweed
Drawings reproduced by Chatsworth Studios
Printed by Martin's of Berwick

CONTENTS

Acknowledgements

I wish to thank most warmly the many people who have helped me towards the publication of my 'odyssey'. I look back with pleasure to their kindly guidance.

The beautiful drawings by James Alder have greatly enhanced my story, and I am grateful for his collaboration in other aspects of its production.

I owe Sir Peter Scott my warmest thanks for his encouragement and kindly criticism, and for his shining example as a master of his art.

George Wall was one of my companions on most of these expeditions – I could not have wanted a better man. Besides his great knowledge of European birds and wide experience in wildlife photography, he was resourceful and unflappable in all crises.

FOREWORD

Sir James Steel has had a lifelong interest in natural history, especially in ornithology. He has also travelled in over a hundred different countries. In many of these he went on expeditions with one or more artists or scientists to observe, photograph, and film wild birds.

The field notes he made on those expeditions are the subject of this book, which provides a first-hand record of the experiences of a keen observer of rare birds in their natural environment. Some of these notes have been used in preparing lectures to many Natural History Societies, or in writing the sound tracks for his films which have been widely shown.

This is not a scientific book but it will be a delight to anyone who is interested in the fascinating study of birds. The author invites us to share something of the joys, thrills and frustrations of close contact with many rarities in a wide variety of habitats.

Sir James has become very knowledgeable over his years of bird photography, and I count myself lucky indeed to have been associated with him in the development of the Wildfowl Trust Centre at Washington which he guided so effectively for fifteen years from the time of its first conception in 1972 and which has been enjoyed by nearly a million visitors to date.

Sir Peter Scott CH CBE DSC FRS

Slimbridge 1988

INTRODUCTION

More a Way of Life

I discovered the world of birds when I was aged between four and five years, staying with my mother and a younger sister on holiday at Great Broughton, in the North Riding of Yorkshire.

I had climbed a small tree in a nearby lane. As I descended I came level with the mud-lined nest of a Song Thrush, containing four sky-blue eggs freckled with black spots. Of course, I did not know they were Song Thrush's eggs, but I knew I had found a wonderful treasure. Without any feeling of guilt, I took one to show my mother, carried it in my cupped hands with infinite care and no small triumph. Gentle soul that she was, my mother explained that my theft of an egg would cause much grief to the parent birds and end the life of an embryo chick, which would within a few weeks have become another lovely speckled thrush to delight our eyes and our ears with its musical whistling.

I decided there and then never to take another bird's egg. Nor have I done. In those far-off days every boy at some stage of his career collected birds' eggs and few adults thought it a crime. On his arrival at the week-end, my father took a more pragmatic view as it was then too late to return the egg to the nest; he showed me how to blow it with a pin hole at each end, so that it might be kept safely. But he gave me no encouragement to create a collection.

In the same holiday I leaned over the parapet of the stone bridge at Stokesley. A Kingfisher flew under it at that very moment in a flash of blue and went away down the river. This lovely vision, which is still bright in my memory, confirmed my decision never to hunt or destroy any bird. Many times in later life I have watched and filmed kingfishers driving their nest holes into the clay bank of a stream or bringing minnows in their red bills to feed their young; but none have exceeded that first thrilling sight.

Both at my school in Nottinghamshire and in my home county Durham, there was always a fine variety of birds to watch and identify in a wide choice of habitats. Species seemed more plentiful then: four species of owls, for example, the Barn, Tawny, Little and Short-eared, were always to be found where I knew they habitually nested close to my home. When I think of the early mornings of the long summer days at school in the Midlands, it is chiefly the insistent call of the Corncrake that I remember; but I never saw it; it skulked in the long grass and never showed itself.

My first attempt to photograph any bird was not at all successful. This was in the garden of a week-end cottage which my mother owned at Worton in Wensleydale. A pair of Blue Tits was obligingly rearing a family in a nesting box close by a ground-floor window and I thought this would provide a perfect subject. They would not come to the nest with me in sight so I took my pictures from the window eight feet away. With my Brownie box camera this gave too small an image. So I fastened the camera to a post at a distance of three feet and operated the shutter with a length of thread from the window. But my reflex was too slow. The parent had always popped into the hole or emerged from it before I had operated the shutter.

From that bungled attempt I graduated to the use of a hide. I discovered by experiment that elaborate camouflage is not needed so long as the operator is hidden from the bird's view. My first effort did not discourage the Redstarts from returning with food every two or three minutes to their nest hidden in a loose stone wall. With what I thought was split-second timing, I exposed a whole reel of film in my more sophisticated camera. When this was developed I had a series of thirty-six photographs with excellent focus and exposure of a dry-stone wall but no sign of any bird. Their movements were too fast.

After trying with flash and then making the flying bird break an 'electric-eye' beam with only moderate success, I decided to concentrate on 'movie' to film birds in action. I purchased a second-hand Bolex camera and gained my experience with it.

During the next twenty years I had limited opportunity to watch or film natural history subjects at home and none at all overseas. Although during those years I encircled the world several times in planes and visited a hundred and two different countries in the course of my business in engineering, these visits left no time for bird-watching or, indeed for any other hobbies.

Glimpses of strange birds seen from plane windows on take-off or landing excited my ambition to make a detailed study at a later date. I never even took my binocular on these journeys because I knew I should have no time to use it. On car journeys between cities I often saw eagles, buzzards and vultures and occasionally pelicans soaring on a thermal or storks on migration passage, but these are only glimpses and not bird-watching.

In the years when I was so often abroad I took every opportunity to watch and film most of our local birds in Upper Weardale. This provides a variety of habitats – streams, lakes, forests, marsh and moorland, all richly endowed with bird species. The numbers are now much reduced and a few species are missing entirely, such as the Barn Owl, which always bred near us. One vivid memory is of a Short-eared Owl which I had been filming as it fed its young among the heather. I was satisfied with some excellent shots taken from a hide just twelve feet away. As I had entered the hide unobserved and the hen showed no alarm at the sound of the camera, I soon had all the footage I wanted. I packed up my equipment and made ready to leave the hide whilst both parents were hunting. I was kneeling on the ground at the back of the hide, lacing up the backcloth when the male bird returned and struck my back a heavy blow with its claws. These fastened on my leather jacket but drew no blood. The attack was called off as soon as I stood up. I had to admire the courage it exhibited in attacking an intruder so much bigger than itself. This incident did not disturb the birds unduly as they successfully reared the chicks, after which I removed the hide. It is a lovely sight to watch this bird hunting low over the heather in broad daylight.

Another predator which nests among the heather is the smallest of our falcons, the Merlin, and I am lucky to have this increasingly rare bird of prey breeding every year near to my home. The nest is well concealed amongst tall heather but the three or four young disperse nearby soon after hatching and only come together to be fed. Watching the parents hunting Meadow Pipits on the moors, one soon sees a kill taken to the 'killing stone' where the prey is torn to pieces. The young are then always close by and clamouring to be fed. If the hide is erected and entered discreetly the parents ignore it.

It is not so much fun when one is regarded as potential quarry being hunted rather than being the hunter, although I only hunt with a camera. I was lying on my back high up on the fells watching a Common Buzzard as it circled in decreasing gyres far above me. Suddenly it stooped at me as if it saw in me a potential meal, so I scrambled to my feet. It immediately swooped upwards and away. The buzzard has such magnificent eyesight that I could hardly believe it mistook me for a hare. Later I learned that a young buzzard fallen from the nest had been taken to a bird-lover in the area who had reared it in captivity, to be later released into the wild. I concluded that this was the bird which has seen me and approached for a closer look at the man who might have proved to be its trusted friend.

We have Greater Spotted Woodpeckers, Nuthatches and other interesting species coming regularly to our birdtable in winter, Crossbills to our pine trees and Hen Harriers to our moors, but these are common enough in some parts of Britain. A fall of Waxwings is not unusual in their winter migration from Scandinavia every autumn. We are lucky to see most of the migrants passing through. In recent years we have had 'accidentals' such as the Hoopoe and the Roller but I like to watch these further south now that I have time to go where they are quite common.

Certainly I have missed chances of seeing birds never found in the U.K. but common enough in their native countries where I was a frequent visitor but always in too much of a hurry. One incident in the Arabian Gulf area stays in my memory because I actually had the bird in my hand. I was walking in a street in Daman in Saudi Arabia when I was approached by three young Saudis who carried a wicker cage containing a small bird. This they wanted to sell to me and the price they asked for bird and cage was reasonable, so I bought it. It was obviously one of the

Waxbills but I could not tell which because it had no distinctive colouring about the head which would have identified its species. It was probably a female, being a mottled brown overall, except for its bright red bill. Having examined its feathering, I opened the cage door and let it fly free. I returned the empty cage to its owners with thanks. Clearly they thought I was mad and made haste to put a safe distance between us. I often wondered if they baited the cage and caught the same bird again. If so, they would certainly have looked around for another lunatic to pay good money and let the captive fly free.

I am content now to remain at home to study our resident birds in the changing pageant of the seasons and to watch the ebb and flow of migrants.

The more one learns about birds, the more one wants to know. Like drinking salt water, it increases the thirst it seeks to slake. When once I watched the arrival of our winter visitors, I wanted to see them in their breeding habitat in the high north. When I saw the departure of our summer migrants, I longed to follow them to the sunshine of their winter quarters.

In most years some rarity arrives exhausted on our shores; it has been blown here by contrary winds and stays a few days to feed and rest. News of its arrival spreads instantaneously among birdwatchers; hundreds gather with telescopes and telephoto lens cameras to the dismay of farmers and doubtless of the bird. I have sought such rarities in their native lands, where I could watch and film them unharassed and unafraid.

The following chapters record some of these expeditions I have made with different friends to distant countries and islands. Usually the journey has been made to find and study one or two particular species of bird but always to observe all nature. In drawing upon my notes written in the field, I have experienced anew the thrill of watching rare birds at close quarters, completely undisturbed and behaving quite naturally.

It is easy to see when a bird being watched from a hide is ill at ease and to move the hide to a greater distance if it has been brought too close.

To photograph or film or just to watch birds at close quarters usually requires the use of a hide. This need not be elaborately camouflaged but should be of a neutral colour. Rubber bands, cut from old tyre inner tubes, stretched around each of three sides of canvas and at three levels facilitate the insertion of local vegetation to soften the outline.

To plan such an operation one must identify the site to which the subject will come. This is most often a nest but it may also be a singing perch, a bathing pool, a favourite preening site, a drinking place, or a regularly used source of food or nest material. Some species use a chosen site, known as a lek, to display or dance or fight, to attract the attention of the hen birds.

Birds observed at the nest may be feeding young, or incubating eggs, or even building the nest, the latter being the most difficult of all to film because birds are then most wary unless the site is inaccessible.

The placing of the hide should always follow the same procedure, avoidance of disturbance to the subject taking precedence over the achievement of a quick result or an outstanding picture. Having ascertained that the subject is absent from the chosen site, the birdwatcher erects his hide quickly at a considerable distance from the site. This distance varies with the species of bird. For a ground-nesting bird of timid disposition, such as a Curlew, it might be fifty metres. For a bolder bird with its nest in a hedge, such as a Linnet, it might be ten metres. The reaction of the bird to the empty hide should then be observed through a binocular from a distance and preferably from a car or other shelter. If there is no hesitation by the bird in returning to the site, it has accepted the sudden appearance in its environment of a strange but apparently harmless object. If it will not readily return, the hide is too near or too obtrusive and must be moved back and better camouflaged.

After the lapse of twenty-four hours the hide may be moved closer with the same avoidance of distress to the bird. One may halve the intervening distance and again watch from afar the returning subject's behaviour. With another day's delay the hide may be moved forward again, halving the distance as before; the reaction of the bird is again observed from a distance and the hide is moved back if its presence is not readily accepted. It is no longer necessary to photograph or film at very close quarters: the high quality of telephoto and zoom lenses now facilitates excellent close-up pictures from a fair distance.

In some situations, such as a cliff ledge or high tree, there may be only a single possible location for the hide. In such a situation the hide must be built in stages and of local materials, if practicable, or be well camouflaged. There should be three or four stages with twenty-four hour intervals and distant observation between each.

All this cautious behaviour is not so wasteful of time if three or four subjects and sites are being worked simultaneously with a sufficiency of hides.

These are the procedures my friends and I have used on many expeditions with fair success, little or no disturbance to wildlife and much healthy enjoyment.

These are not scientific reports but they may have some value as first-hand records of observations made in the field. Their main purpose is to share the pleasure these expeditions gave to my companions and me. No precise locations are given of nest sites because too often the publication of expedition reports with map references are followed by predatory raids of oologists.

Gyr-falcon

CHAPTER ONE

The Boreal Island

The joyless news reached us on the high seas. We were bound for
Reykjavik out of Leith in that fine ship *Gullfoss* and the knell of
fate warned us that the stevedores were on strike and the *Gullfoss*
would be unable to discharge her cargo. I broke the news to my
two friends, George and Harvey, in their cabin, where they were
still seeking their sea legs and then I went to the saloon to discuss
the rumour with other passengers.

There were birds to be watched on board ship; Gannets high
diving, Fulmars floating on the airslip, Herring Gulls, Blackbacks
and the Common Gull. As we approached Iceland, a Great Skua
passed us on some piratical errand and a Wheatear, too far from
land, came to rest on the ship's rail. They were small consolation.
Our thoughts were set upon the rare birds of Iceland we had
planned in such detail to see – the White-tailed Eagle, the Snowy
Owl, and, most desirable of all, the Gyrfalcon.

I visited the captain for authentic information. He told me that
the strike continued and the two sides stood firm. The ship would
be tied up alongside to allow passengers to disembark; they could
take ashore only hand luggage; no cargo could be discharged. She
would then be moved from her berth to lie at anchor in the roads
for two days until due to sail. If the strike was still on, she would
move back to her berth for half an hour only to take on board new
passengers with hand luggage.

What about our Landrover containing all our expedition
equipment and which had been carried as deck cargo, I asked.

The captain shook his head. 'That will have to remain on board
and I shall put it ashore at Leith.'

The Landrover was new and equipped for rough terrain travel:
power steering, stone guards, a winch, and extra fuel tanks. It had
a special body with sleeping bunks, gas cooking and water
heating, and fly-proof screens. It was stocked with basic food for

a month, medical equipment and all our photographic and sound-recording gear. Without it we might as well return home with the ship. Our annual leave and months of planning and preparation would be wasted.

We came alongside on 7th June; the ship was moored fore and aft and the gangway lowered. A picket line blocked the shore end of the pier. All disembarking passengers had been warned to take ashore only hand luggage. We three each carried a rucksack on our back and a box under each arm, but around our necks we had hung cameras, binoculars, telephoto lenses and every piece of equipment that had a strap on it. They smiled and let us through.

Behind the rope barrier I saw a man I knew. I had apprised him of our arrival date and there he was, with true Icelandic hospitality, at the end of the pier to meet us. He proved to be a friend indeed. He took us in his car to an excellent hotel where he had reserved rooms for us and there he expounded his plan. If the strike broke within two days, the *Gullfoss* would return to her berth and discharge her cargo, including our precious vehicle and our half ton of stores and equipment. If not, they would all go back to Leith. Meanwhile, we could see our Consul and also meet the strike committee to attempt to persuade the stevedores to bring our Landrover ashore.

If all our blandishments failed, he had arranged for us to hire an ex-American army four-wheel drive, cross-country personnel carrier and a tent; it was equipped with radio, which he thought essential so that we could call for help if we broke down or were stuck in any of the deserts or swamps we would have to cross. It was one thing we had not thought about. We were immensely grateful.

The Consul was sympathetic but could give no help. Twice we had an audience of the strike committee, to appeal on the grounds that ours was a scientific expedition and not a mere holiday, but its members were unmoved. Had it not been so frustrating, I would have enjoyed the experience; the committee occupied the first floor rooms of a small office block; they were crowded with men all talking at once; the tables were covered with beer bottles, empty or in noisy process of being emptied.

Three or four men at a time were always shouting down telephones. Our friend interpreted for us. It was difficult in these circumstances to present a logical argument and withers seemed unwrung. However, they did make us a valuable concession, as we later learned.

We occupied the first day of waiting by exploring on foot this modern and attractive capital city. Everywhere there is water but trees are almost completely missing. The old town surrounding the harbour is colourful and has a freshwater lake rich in Eider Duck, Arctic Terns, Mallard and Tufted Duck, Black-headed and Glaucous Gulls. In the parks we saw a Redwing nesting – the smallest of our thrushes with a streaked breast and a white eyebrow stripe. I never found it nesting at home although it does occasionally breed in Scotland. It comes to us in the autumn in small numbers amid much larger flocks of Fieldfares. It was good to see it at close quarters quite unafraid on its mud-lined nest incubating sky-blue eggs.

In the parks we watched Redshank, Pied Wagtails, Ringed Plovers, and Rock Pipits. There was plenty for a bird watcher to see without leaving Reykjavik. But our minds were fixed on more exciting species.

The photographing and filming of rare birds at their nests in Iceland is prohibited by the Ministry of Culture & Education without prior permission having been obtained on recommendation of the Bird Protection Committee. I had earlier written to the chairman of that committee, Dr Finnur Gudmundsson, to whom I had an introduction through a common friend. We visited the Ministry where we had an interesting meeting. Regulations had been tightened due to abuse by many egg-collectors and now permits were rarely being given.

We were favoured with a permit to photograph and film the Gyrfalcon but not the Eagles or Owls or Little Auks. We learned that it would be difficult to find any Gyrfalcons breeding this year. These birds feed chiefly on Ptarmigan and the numbers of Ptarmigan vary in cycles, of which the cause is unknown. This year was a low Ptarmigan year, they told us. The Ministry had mounted a special study to discover the cause of the low breeding

Redwing

years but it had not yet reached any conclusion. They told us that the traditional nesting sites were unoccupied this year. We pulled out our large-scale map whereon we had marked fifteen well-known Gyrfalcon nest sites derived from our reading of earlier naturalists' reports. The Gyrfalcon, like most raptors, uses several favoured nest sites in succession so that each may be rid of parasites before its next occupation. They feared all these would be found empty but thought it well for us to check. They asked us to report on them when we returned to Reykjavik and also to give them news of any sightings of the rare Gyrfalcon, about whose status they expressed concern.

Twenty-four hours of daylight provided time also for some tourist sight-seeing. Gullfoss, the Golden Waterfall, after which the ship is named, had to be admired. It falls 200 metres with a right-angled turn and then plunges into a deep gorge. To my mind it appeared more spectacular than either Victoria or Niagara.

The Great Geyser is the spouting hot-spring after which all others throughout the world are so named. It no longer frequently gushes, exhausted perhaps by performing for eager tourists, but we visited to pay homage and to see the hot sulphurous pools and boiling mud in the vicinity. There are other less famous geysers nearby and one of these obligingly spouted water and steam when we primed it with a bar of soap.

In roadside pools we watched Red-necked Phalaropes and Purple Sandpipers and admired the dancing flight of the Snow-bunting, singing as it descended.

A boy entering a farm house stopped to show us an egg he was carrying. George identified this as the egg of the Black-tailed Godwit and showed him a coloured illustration of the bird in our field guide which he agreed was the author of his egg. This species winters along the shores of Britain but breeds only in south eastern Europe and the Middle East and, curiously, in the south western corner of Iceland. We were keen to film the parent birds at the nest but the boy was reluctant to show us where he had found it. Maybe he felt guilty for having taken one of these rare eggs.

We were within sight of the Langjokull glacier which we

examined through field glasses; we would have plenty opportunities of closer acquaintance with glaciers further north. Dominating the skyline was the volcano Hekla, now in rather mild eruption. We determined to test the cross-country performance of our hired vehicle by approaching as near to it as we dared.

By devious routes over solidified lava and volcanic ash we came alarmingly close to the mouth of the volcano. Large and small rocks were being hurled to a great height so we left the vehicle out of range and approached nearer on foot to film and photograph. The eruption was continuous but inconsistent, the more violent emissions being unpredictable. It was all accompanied by a great deal of noise as of the banging together of thousands of steel plates. A flow of red hot lava crept down the slope from an opening below the crater rim. It turned black quite soon but kept on moving inexorably. I could imagine the horror of any threatened village in the path of such a flow.

On our return journey we turned aside to see the Althing at Thingvellis, the site of the ancient parliament, founded, I was told, in the early tenth century A.D. and thus the oldest of parliaments. There was not much to see: an open space by a lake, the Lögberg or Rock of the Law, a narrow valley where the horses were tethered. The Thing was held once a year or when needed: it lasted for a few days. Each chieftain set up his 'booth' where he left behind his weapons before going into session – a necessary precaution to avoid bloodshed.

I was given two examples of these ancient laws which seemed to me eminently sensible: an early Icelander claiming virgin land to enclose for farming had to light a wood fire at each of its four corners and keep them all burning for twenty-four hours. This prevented a man from being too greedy. A widow who inherited her husband's land was allowed to keep only such an area as she could walk a cow around in a day.

We took a brief look at the whaling station on the outskirts of Reykjavik. One man was flensing a whale with a long-handled knife but his work was almost finished and I could not recognise the species. It was nauseating and I had no desire to prolong the visit. How tragic it is that we still destroy these splendid mammals; I believe about 400 are killed each year around Iceland.

The *Gullfoss* was due to sail the following morning without discharging her cargo. On returning to our hotel we received the welcome news of a concession to us by the strike committee. The three of us could go out on the pilot's cutter when he went aboard to bring the ship alongside its berth. Whilst anchor was weighed and she was being brought by tugs to her moorings we could empty our Landrover and move the contents to the ship's rail. She would lie at the quayside for less than half an hour whilst passengers and their hand luggage came up the gangway, during which time we could put our belongings over the side onto the quay.

Never did stevedores work so hard as we did! We emptied the Landrover as the ship was brought to the quay and we had all our stores landed before she was ready to sail. Then we manhandled our gear through the picket line and into our waiting vehicle. We did not fail to thank the strikers although we had little sympathy for them. We were sad indeed to see our Landrover sail, taking with it our high hopes of a comfortable bed each night and some haute cuisine cooking. I never did learn how the strike ended and whether all the harassment was worth the stevedores' while.

We should have left immediately our stores were loaded but we decided to have lunch at the hotel where we could entertain our good friend who had helped us so much.

At that last civilised meal we felt like those voyagers who were detained by the 'mild-eyed melancholy lotus-eaters' with flowers and fruit upon the yellow sand and were persuaded to roam no more, and we resisted the temptation! Before leaving we were approached by two Englishmen who had learned we were driving to Akureyri. Could we give them a lift? Their car also had been left aboard the *Gullfoss* and was even now on its way back to Scotland. We had no wish to accommodate two extra passengers but we agreed to take them along.

There is no problem in finding the route to Akureyri for there is only one road. A few miles out of Reykjavik it ceased to present a smooth tarred surface and became an obstacle track of boulders, potholes and deep ruts. We had been warned that the annual road repairs had not been carried out and much of the carriageway had been washed out by spring floods. We might expect potholes. We did, but not the gaping chasms which sometimes drove us off the road to make a detour and sometimes tested our rugged vehicle and our own less-rugged frames to the limit.

Our destination lay on the northern coast some 322 kilometres distant. With twenty-four hours of daylight we had no scheduled time for arrival; we proceeded quite leisurely, taking turns at driving. We had not travelled far before we were flagged down by a girl on the roadside. She spoke English and sought our help. She and her husband had driven a hundred metres off the road towards the coast and now found the surface too soft to drive up the slight incline back to the road. This was the moment to test more rigorously the performance of our machine on soft ground.

We attached the tow rope and engaged the four-wheel drive; the wheels spun in the soft mud surface; we stopped at once to avoid digging a grave and slipped back a few metres onto fresh ground; we adopted the well-known device of letting some air out of the tyres. With the girl at the wheel of the car and the redoubtable George at the wheel of our vehicle and by taking a gentler slope, we slowly drew the offending car back onto the road with five strong men pushing behind. They were extremely grateful and Icelandic/British relations were never better despite fishing disputes.

We resumed our journey with the road becoming progressively worse. We felt no sense of urgency and stopped at roadside pools, each one of which had its pair of Red-necked Phalaropes. This beautiful little wader is seen only in winter on our British shores when its vivid spring plumage has changed to grey. It swims on shallow water in a very buoyant manner like a celluloid duck in a baby's bath. When feeding, it often spins rapidly in a tight circle, the object of which is evidently to stir up invertebrates from the bottom of the pool.

The Icelandic name for this bird is Ooinshani but we have no name in our own vernacular, the English word being taken from its scentific name *Phalaropus*. Oddly enough this is itself erroneous because it should be spelled Phalaridopus from the two Greek words *phalaridos* and *pous*, meaning 'coot foot'. This has reference to the toes of the Phalarope which are lobed, as are those of the Coot. The Red-necked Phalarope has the specific scientific name of Lobatus from the Greek *lobos*, whose meaning is obvious, whereas the Grey Phalarope is distinguished by the specific name Fulicarius from the Latin word for a Coot, thus the scientific and specific names are identical.

Another peculiarity of this delightful bird is the male's obligatory incubation duties; hence it is more sombrely coloured than the female. Whereas in photography of most wildlife the problem is to approach sufficiently close to obtain a good picture, the problem with the Phalarope in its breeding area is to move the tripod far enough away from the subject. Both cock and hen insist on foraging around the photographer's feet; when chased away, they return immediately. I suppose our feet stir up insects from the vegetation.

We continued on our way to Akureyri, taking turns at the driving wheel. George proved to be the most adept at taking the pot holes and trenches at an angle to avoid bottoming the springs and we found ourselves giving him the longest stints. By the time the day was far spent and the sun had dipped to the horizon – but never below it – George was driving continuously. This is a raw, elemental and colourful land. Up to 11,000 years ago it was completely covered with ice. Even now large areas lie beneath the biggest glaciers in Europe. It is sparsely populated outside of the two towns. Twice we stopped at roadside cafés to buy refreshment but they were closed. I had read that eighty percent of the land area of Iceland is uninhabited and our drive from south to north confirmed this; half of the country's people live in the capital. On this journey we saw no cultivation other than grass. The farms were widely scattered and devoted mainly to sheep rearing. There were small numbers of shorthorn cattle in some fields and occasionally we saw little herds of the attractive brown and white Icelandic ponies, often with foals at foot.

Iceland is virtually devoid of trees except for occasional dwarf birch and willow. In the ninth and tenth centuries, when it was

Raven

settled by Norse Vikings, it was said to be covered with birch forest but glaciers, volcanoes and the love of Vikings for roaring fires completely de-forested the land. This would affect both the climate and the wildlife. I believe there is now a plan of re-afforestation; all the mainland lies just outside the Arctic Circle and trees of the hardier species should grow quite well. Although historically and politically Iceland is very mature, it is geologically and biologically still young: a land in the making.

Rugged mountains of basalt fretted the skyline and snow lay on the high tops which reach to nearly 2,000 metres but the valleys were green and pleasant. We saw one farmer drive his tractor into a field to start turning hay shortly after midnight; normal hours of work are disregarded!

Although we had intended to stop at Akureyri, the continuous light tempted us to by-pass it and press on to Myvatn. We crossed some deep valleys where the going was hazardous in the extreme and saw many birds; but we did not delay to watch them – Arctic Skua, Whimbrel, Black-tailed Godwit, Raven, Redshank and Golden Plover. Birds were active throughout the twenty-four hours.

We were much intrigued by the apparent anxiety of our two passengers to arrive at their destination without delay. If they could reach a small summer hotel at the north-east end of the lake, they told us, they could hire transport to Achteve, their objective – a fishing lodge in the far north-east of the country. They were a strange pair and very secretive: we speculated privately on the true nature of their mission, whether international espionage or commercial exploitation of some rare mineral. But they stuck to their fishing story and would not be shaken. One was very much the dominant character who spoke for both. He knew the area well and we were glad of his guidance. He assured us of a good bath and a meal at the summer hotel before we chose a place to camp.

After negotiating the deep valleys with George apparently tireless at the wheel, we approached the lake Myvatn from the south west. The sight of the lava rock formations compelled us to stop and wonder. Arising from shallow water are numerous castles, turrets, spires and bridges left by lava flow and carved into grotesque shapes by wind and weather during 3,000 eventful years.

And here we had our first sight of the Gyrfalcon which we had travelled so far to watch and to film. It was perched on a finger of rock and allowed us to approach quite close before we stopped our vehicle and, of course, remained in it. It was a male bird, a tiercel; the term 'falcon' is reserved for the female and the smaller male is a 'tiercel'. He looked superb, very proud, very fierce.

Of all birds of prey the Gyrfalcon is supreme, the noblest in appearance, the swiftest in flight, the deadliest in attack. Falconers were used to distinguish between three races of the Gyrfalcon – the Icelandic they considered to be of the greatest courage, the fastest, and the most lethal in its stoop. It was prized by falconers above all others and reserved in medieval times exclusively to kings.

There is an ancient order of precedence for the proper use of falcons: Eagles are for emperors; Gyrfalcons for kings; Peregrines for princes; Sakers for knights; Merlins for ladies; Goshawks for yeomen; Sparrowhawks for priests; Muskets (the male Sparrowhawk) for a 'holy water clerk' and Kestrels for knaves. Falcons are so called from the Latin word *falx*, meaning a sickle, because of the bill which is shaped like one. They are all dark-eyed and long-winged predators whereas hawks have rounded wings and yellow eyes.

Some of these magnificent birds are almost pure white in colour but this tiercel was a darker morph. The plumage of the nape and back was dark grey barred with white and the breast was pale cream flecked with black; it had a dark moustachial stripe less prominent than that of the peregrine, and large dark eyes. It took off before we had looked our fill.

We chose the road south of Myvatn and reached the summer hotel which provided the promised good meal. Before leaving, our knowledgeable passenger volunteered to show us where we could have a hot bath and we never ceased to be grateful to him for this. Following a rough track, we were guided to a cave leading down to an underground river which flowed within a lava pipe. The water was at exactly the right temperature for a bath and we lost no time in entering it.

The pool was about four metres wide and two metres deep; the water flowed quite swiftly for about twenty metres before the roof became too low to swim on the surface. We swam in that luxurious bath at some time on every day whilst we stayed at Myvatn. We learned later that the temperature never varies more than a degree celsius up or down in winter and summer.

Our camp was pitched in the foothills two kilometres north-east of the lake beside a small tarn. There was no wood for a fire and our cooking was by Calor gas; the tarn provided water for drinking and washing; the tent we used only for sleeping. Theoretically we took turns in cooking but George had a unique facility for producing hot soup or tea within minutes of our return, cold, tired or wet from long hours of bird watching; so that, in the event, he did far more than his share. Harvey and I manifested our skill at washing up. Because of continuous daylight we ignored conventional hours, ate when we were famished and slept when we could keep awake no longer.

On our first day we explored Myvatn by circumnavigation, the track along the north-west shore being much rougher than the road on the south-east. The area of the lake is thirty-eight square kilometres and it is very shallow with many small islands. In summer time it is estimated that up to 150,000 ducks are feeding and breeding there. The water is rich in ammonia, warmed by hot springs, and its depth of up to three metres allows the sun to develop bottom vegetation as well as abundance of plankton. No shooting is permitted and fish abound; it is a paradise for fishermen and for the fish-eating Mergansers and Goosanders. The local farmers crop the eggs; up to 50,000 may be collected in a season with only a few taken from each nest so that the duck does not desert.

It is the meeting place of temperate and frigid zones and it lies midway between Europe and North America. It is the northern breeding limit for many birds from Europe and Africa and the southern limit for the arctic birds. Hence its great ornithological interest.

We visited all the Gyrfalcon breeding sites in the area which we had recorded on our maps; all were on south-facing cliffs and readily identifiable by the white-wash of droppings below the ledge; but we found none in use save one. To reach this we travelled across a desert of grey volcanic ash. The wheels often started to spin even with the four-wheel drive engaged; then we stopped at once and reversed along our tracks until we reached firmer ground; we searched on foot for a more solid route.

We found the nest in a horizontal cleft in the rock on the steep side of a shallow valley. It measured about half a metre in diameter, made of sticks and covered with Ptarmigan feathers. There were two eggs in it which were very cold, originally white but now discoloured by a covering of snow. Around the nest were a few wings and bones of Ptarmigan. The parent Falcons were not in the area. We concluded that the hen bird had sat for several weeks on sterile eggs and then deserted the nest. We took one egg which we later handed in to the Bird Protection Committee representatives in Reykjavik for analysis to learn if the sterility was due to mercuric or other toxic inclusion derived through the food chain.

Harvey, whose keen eyes often located nests, found a pair of Slavonian Grebes – sometimes named the Horned Grebe – with a floating nest of vegetation amongst the reeds near the shore. We put up a hide and gradually advanced it to within six metres whence we had an excellent view of the nest and sat up to the waist in warm water. The male bird sometimes brought an offering of vegetation which the female built into the nest. Once the male also clambered onto the bulky nest and mated with her. He was constantly swimming nearby and made a colourful picture with a gold eye-stripe leading up to the 'horns' above his black head. The neck and sides were coloured a rich chestnut in his breeding plumage.

The Whimbrel is quite common all over the lower ground of Iceland, nesting in boggy areas. It is only a rare visitor to Britain where non-breeding birds may occasionally be seen on our shores in summer time. It breeds circumpolar at high latitudes and winters as far south as the equator where it frequents the seashore

Slavonian Grebe

in many countries. George found the nest of a pair which we were able to film without any difficulty. The four eggs must have been near to hatching because the hen returned to her nest the moment one of us had entered the hide.

This was a splendid opportunity to study a normally shy bird through a binocular at about six metres' distance and to admire its boldly striped head and long de-curved bill. It is smaller and more slightly built than our familiar Curlew but very similar in colouration. We did not stay too long lest the parent birds should be disturbed.

Another nest we found in the Myvatn district was that of the Snow Bunting. It had made a neat little nest lined with white feathers in a hole in the lava rock. It was placed about 300 millimetres from the entrance and we could only film the two adult birds flitting around outside, which they did somewhat nervously. There were six eggs in the nest but we left it quickly, being satisfied to watch these dainty birds from a distance in their smart black and white summer plumage. We see them sometimes in winter in their duller winter dress.

One bird we had hoped to film was the Great Northern Diver, which is an occasional winter visitor to our coastal sea but breeds only in the high north. Harvey found a nest on a grassy promontory in a small lake north-west of Myvatn; it was a flat nest of aquatic vegetation only a few centimetres above the water. We established two hides on the shore to film across eighteen metres of lake from two different angles with 640 mm lenses. The female left the nest to feed and there was no problem in erecting the hides in the high vegetation on the lake shore without disturbing her. She appeared to ignore them completely on her return for they were well hidden.

She left the nest very smoothly by slipping on breast and belly down a short slide into the water, but her return was most ungainly. She waddled with obvious difficulty up the slope on short legs set too far back for walking but good for swimming.

The Great Northern Diver is nearly as large as a domestic goose and very beautiful in its handsome black and white breeding plumage. The head is glossy black, the breast a vivid

Whimbrel

white, and the wings and back chequered black and white. The neck has a collar of vertical black and white stripes. This pattern of colours and its large size make this a glorious bird to watch and to film. The male only appeared occasionally but kept in vocal contact. The call of one parent answering the other over a distance is most memorable; it is a loud and weird sound that has been variously described as 'wailing' and 'laughter'. To me it seemed one of the loneliest sounds one could hear, ringing across this deserted wetland with a haunting sorrow.

The bird's name in Canada, the Loon, is generally thought to be named after this weird call. But Yarrel wrote in 1843 that all the four species of diver in Europe were known as Loon or Loom. This comes from a Lap word *lumme* meaning lame because the family of divers has so awkward a gait on land. The Norwegian name is Lom, the Great Northern Diver being Storlom and the Red-throated Diver, Smalom, signifying Great and Small Divers respectively.

The two eggs in this nest were olive coloured and as big as swan's eggs. She would leave them for half an hour at a time to feed, when she swam near at hand and made sudden dives to re-appear at considerable distances. She had also the ability to swim almost submerged with just the head and neck above water. Once she flew, rising from the water with apparent difficulty and much paddling of the feet. When airborne, however, she flew very strongly but her return to the water was a heavy splash-down.

Each time we approached a hide we battled through a dense cloud of flies hanging over the vegetation like smoke. Our feet stirred even more from the low bushes until one feared to breathe; we understood very well why the lake is named Myvatn, meaning the 'lake of midges'. They are of two kinds, Simulidae and Chironomidae, which we knew as the 'black' and the 'grey' midges. Often the lenses of our cameras were so obscured by clouds of these insects that we would no longer take photographs until they had settled. Happily human skin held no attraction for them and we suffered no bites or physical irritation. There are reports of visitors to Myvatn having become so alarmed by these suffocating clouds that they ran back to their cars without waiting to see all the glories of the lake.

Here, indeed, ducks abound and all fifteen species may be observed in the space of an hour. One of my favourites is the Longtail, known in North America as the 'Old Squaw'. Its cry is musical and quite unlike the quack of our farmyard duck. I intercepted one of these ducks as it waddled back to the lake and picked it up without difficulty; it lay quiescent in my arms without fear whilst my companions photographed us. the freedom from shooting justifies their trust. Scaup were very plentiful as were also Mallard, Teal and Wigeon – all ducks common enough at home. The elegant Pintail and the colourful Shovellers are no rarity either but the Barrow's Goldeneye differs in appearance from our European Goldeneye in the D-shaped white patch behind the eye in place of the familiar circular patch. This is the only place in Europe where this North American bird is found. It is named after Sir John Barrow of the British Admiralty and founder of the Royal Geographical Society.

We searched for and duly found another duck, the Harlequin, which breeds in Iceland but is only vagrant to the rest of Europe. They were enjoying the swift white water of the Laxa river where it flows out of Myvatn. How they can swim upstream against such a turbulent current is a mystery but the rougher the water the more they appear to enjoy it. The drake has dark blue plumage on the head and back with chestnut on the flanks. The white spots and streaks on the breast, neck and head give it the pantomime appearance which justifies its name and match its playful antics in the water.

Gadwall, Pochard and Tufted together with large numbers of Common Scoters made up the tally of species of the true ducks. We watched and filmed also the sawtooth ducks – Red-breasted Mergansers and Goosanders, which catch fish underwater and make their nests in holes in the lava rock.

Harvey found a nest of the Common Snipe with two chicks just hatching. An hour later he looked again and these precocial young had already left the parental home but he located them crouching in a scrape on the ground nearby. We found four nests of the Red-necked Phalarope well hidden amongst reeds at the

Long-tailed Duck

edges of pools. One contained four eggs and others each three.

As we were driving near to a small lake north of Myvatn we watched a game of swans circling and descending. Our field glasses revealed them to be Whooper Swans, very similar in shape and colouring to the Bewick but larger. Size is relative and without seeing the two species together it is not easy to distinguish between them. The tip of the black and yellow bill to the top of the head forms a straight line in both but the yellow part of the bill of the Whooper extends beyond the nostril but in the Bewick it stops short of it. Both have straight necks at rest (unlike the familiar curved neck of the Mute) but the neck of the Whooper at the bottom lies back upon the body before assuming the vertical whereas in the Bewick it goes straight up. We counted twenty, including five juveniles which had not yet lost their grey plumage.

We put up tripods and filmed them landing on the lake. This was an exhilarating sight; they lined up before coming in and landed at a considerable speed, throwing up a bow wave. As they came to rest, their heads went down stretching the long necks to reach the bottom vegetation.

They did not feed for long. Whether our presence half a kilometre distant made them nervous or whether the feeding was not to their liking I do not know but within half an hour they began to take off in small groups. The departure was as dramatic as the arrival. Their long wings thrashed the water as they gathered speed to lift their great weight and with loud whooping calls they formed into chevron formation and disappeared over the horizon.

We watched them in awe because these magnificent birds breed in Iceland and most of them migrate to winter in the British Isles, a journey of nearly a thousand kilometres, without a pause to rest or feed. Others breeding in northern Norway winter in Western Europe and yet others breeding in Siberia winter in the areas of the Black Sea, Caspian Sea and Japan. Each group remains faithful to its breeding and wintering grounds. What splendid and reliable birds they are and how sad that many should be shot or die of lead poisoning either from carrying shot or swallowing lead weights lost by fishermen in canals and lakes.

It was time for us to continue our search for the elusive Gyrfalcon. We had closely questioned the local people and the occasional tourist guide whom we met about the possibility of finding a breeding pair of Gyrfalcons. At last we heard a rumour of a nest being occupied in the district of Nordur-thing in the far north-east of Iceland. We were given the name of a blind farmer near Axarfjord who is a fine naturalist and would be sure to know about it.

We set off at once to find him and to look at the famous waterfall Dettafoss on the way. As we left the northern end of Myvatn we saw the relics of sulphur mines which are no longer worked but there were signs of activity in the shallow water of the lake which we were told related to a plan to extract Kieselguhr from the bottom. I hope this commercial activity does not disturb the wildlife. Nearby are numerous small craters, hot springs and other evidence of geothermal activity.

We travelled over quite a good road north and east to meet the Jokulsa river and followed it downstream to the Dettafoss, said to be the largest waterfall in Europe. Following our verbal directions we eventually located the blind farmer who proved to be a most friendly and interesting character. With his knowledge of English much superior to our knowledge of Icelandic and his small residual sight he conveyed to us some part of his vast knowledge of the birds of his country. He showed us the wings of Great Black-backs and other sea birds to demonstrate his points. He described from his own earlier observations how the Gyrfalcon strikes the head of a flying Ptarmigan or duck in its lethal stoop with its two feet clenched together and with such velocity that he had seen the stricken head knocked off with the single blow.

I think he enjoyed the exchange of information and experiences almost as much as we did, despite the difficulty of communication. Downstream of the great waterfall the river flows in a deep gorge. He told us that in his youth there would always be one, and sometimes two pairs of 'falki', as he named the Gyrfalcon, nesting there. He was sad at the diminishing number and had to be reassured that we would only film the birds at the nest if we found one. We then asked him directly if he knew where the pair were breeding in his area. He said there were none or he would have heard of it and he knew all the traditional nest sites for miles around. However, he had heard rumours of a breeding pair in the vicinity of Axarfjord and he gave us the name of the priest there who might be able to help us.

In continuous daylight we drove on and eventually found the priest who spoke excellent English. He was most kind, insisting that we come into his house and share his meal. This we were happy to do, being hungry. The house was solidly stone-built and furnished in a mid-Victorian style. Tea was served with ample bread and jam and cake to which we did full justice. Throughout the meal he plied us with questions and exhibited a good knowledge of current European and world affairs. Finally we worked the conversation round to the Gyrfalcon and, when he had satisfied himself as to our bona fides and had scrutinised our licence to film this rare bird, he promised to help.

He had himself, he told us, no knowledge of the whereabouts of a breeding pair, nor indeed any great interest in ornithology. But he would give us a note to the son of a farmer who would certainly know if the rumour were true. This man does not speak English, he told us, but his note would explain what we are seeking and that we could be trusted. This he did and gave us precise details how to find the farm. We left with mutual expressions of goodwill and a promise to write to him from England.

His directions were good and we found the farm and the man without much trouble but at a greater distance than we had supposed. After reading the priest's note he made it clear that he knew of a pair nesting but thought the young might by now have left the nest. He would lead us to the site. He re-appeared on a tractor and indicated that we should follow him in our vehicle.

We anticipated a rough but short journey as we struck off across the fell without any semblance of a track. We were thankful for the four-wheel drive and good ground clearance which allowed us to follow the tractor. That journey seemed endless; we climbed higher and higher; the scenery became ever more wild; the air grew colder. At last we turned into a narrow valley and followed up a stream. Then the tractor stopped and he signed to us to follow on foot. After 800 metres we approached a great rock outcrop and there he pointed to the nest built in a shallow cave near the top of the cliff and beneath an overhang of rock. Even as we looked through our glasses the falcon shot off the nest and hurtled into the air to watch us from a distance.

Our binoculars now revealed two white eyasses stretching their blue beaks upwards. Our search had ended. We thanked our guide profusely and returned to the vehicles at once, fearing to alarm the falcon, which was watching us from the top of the cliff. We decided to erect our tent at a distance beside our vehicle and to make a plan for filming after we had slept.

Next morning we approached cautiously and in complete silence up the scree which sloped to the foot of the cliff. The falcon flew off and watched us from the cliff top. Through binoculars we could see that she had taken over a Raven's nest for her use, having doubtless driven the unfortunate Raven away. It was a bulky nest of sticks; the Raven must have travelled many miles to collect them in such a tree-less area. There were many feathers all around the nest. We put up our first hide on the scree at about 100 metres from the nest and retired to a distance to watch her come back, which she did within five minutes.

Sunlight did not reach the nest until 11 a.m. and George returned then and shot some film whilst Harvey and I tidied up the camp site. Late in the afternoon we returned to erect the second hide at the top of the scree at half the distance. She was standing on the nest and scolded us severely as we worked but did not fly off. We left her then to become accustomed to the nearer hide and we took still photographs of the many colourful flowers growing among the rocks and gravel. None of us were botanists but we were able to identify some of the plants: lady's bedstraw, thrift, mountain avens, alpine cinquefoil, ladies mantle, thyme, cottongrass and dandelion.

I learned later from a botanist that there are 440 species of native vascular plants in Iceland, of which half are glacial survivors and a third are arctic or alpine species. So we did not botanise very well but we did secure some pretty pictures.

Several hours later we put up the third hide on a rock jutting out from the cliff face at about the same height but some twenty metres to one side of the nest. The falcon did not even leave the site; she had evidently decided we were quite harmless. Up to that time we had not seen the tiercel but just when we had finished we heard him call from a distance and the falcon answered him; the sound of each was a high-pitched scream. We lay down to watch him approach; the falcon flew to meet him and we witnessed the 'food pass' whereby the prey is passed from cock bird to hen in the air, she turning almost upside down to take it. Sadly, we had no camera ready to film it. We retreated to our camp, making plans to spend the whole of the following day in the hides.

As the ever-present sun climbed high enough to reach the cliff we approached it stealthily with all our cameras, tripods, binoculars and spare lenses, including the invaluable zoom lenses and many reels of film. The falcon was standing by the nest so we decided she should not be allowed to see us entering the hides. We waited at some distance to ascertain her pattern of movement. She did not move. For the first hour she only closed her eyes occasionally, the lower lid moving upwards. In the next half-hour she preened in a desultory fashion. The sunlight now being full upon the nest site, we decided to move each into a separate hide and she ignored us completely. From the lowest hide I had a full frontal view and opportunity to study her in detail. She stood nearly upright on one side of the nest. The two eyasses were out of sight, sleeping no doubt in the shallow cup.

Taxonomists used to distinguish between three species of the Gyrfalcon: the Greenland, the Icelandic and the Norwegian, which latter included birds from Sweden and Finland. Now they are all considered to be a single species – *Falco rusticolus* – the Greenland race being generally the largest and the Icelandic larger than the Scandinavian. Our falcon looked at least sixty centimetres from the tip of her blue bill to the end of her long tail. This species comes in three morphs – light, intermediate, and dark; she was of the intermediate morph, being grey in overall colour with a lighter breast flecked with dark brown. The throat and head were white, beautifully marked with the darker shade and a dark moustachial stripe. The tail was a lighter grey with dark brown horizontal bars, the hooked bill was blue and the legs and powerful feet yellow. The eyes were dark brown.

After waiting thus for three hours without the arrival of any food, she suddenly leaned forward and launched herself from the rock platform. Half an hour later the tiercel landed by the nest without food and left again very quickly. We just had time to see he was coloured like the falcon but noticeably smaller; not, however, by as much as a third in our judgement.

Our cameras were loaded and ready; the zoom lenses perfectly focused and the light was good. Only the subject was missing. I remember the words of the High One in the Elder Edda 'the worst sickness of a wise man is to crave what he cannot enjoy'. We seized the chance of the absence of both parent birds to take a closer look at the two eyasses. This involved a scramble up the scree and then in turns a short rock-climb up to the nest where we each shot a reel of movie or took a few stills. We did not prolong our stay because a Gyrfalcon is said to be unafraid of man and is most likely to attack with those deadly talons. We had no inclination to put this theory to the test and each relied upon the others to give plenty of warning if either parent came in sight.

I found the cave quite shallow but the overhang of rock sufficient to give good protection from weather. The nest was a bulky structure of sticks with a wool lining. The two young ones were cream in colour; they lay back with their large yellow feet presenting dangerous black claws in precocious menace. One was slightly larger than the other, although hatching is said to be synchronous. There was no sign of a third egg or dead chick which would have been evident if a normal clutch had been laid. Around the nest was a mass of feathers and the remains of prey picked clean. These showed the food to be almost exclusively Redwing. This confirmed the Ptarmigan shortage and the distance was evidently too great to take duck or sea birds.

We were all back in our hides before the falcon landed with a sudden swoop onto the nest. The young stood up with loud

mewing but she had no food for them. Soon we heard the rattling scream of the tiercel and the falcon flew up to meet him. He slowed almost to a hover with a bird in his talons; she turned on to her back beneath him and snatched the prey from his claws. The pass took only a second so that we had no chance to record it on film before she had swept back to the nest. Standing on its edge, she tore off some feathers to feed strips of flesh first to one and then to the smaller chick. She ate none herself, having probably fed when she went on her solo flight.

Usually the falcon stood on the nest's rim to await the return of the male bird. The intervals between feeding the young varied greatly but the average was about three hours. No large prey was ever brought whilst we were watching; it appears likely that he was only catching passerines at this time. She could hear his cry or see him appear long before we became aware of his approach; sometimes she responded with a more plaintive note.

From our own lofty perch we could see him at a distance of some two kilometres but she could probably see him at twice that distance with her great jewelled eyes. If ours were as big relative to our body mass, they would be as large as saucers.

We filmed them in the air as well as at the nest. They would glide and soar with motionless wings held horizontal and even then their flight was so fast that we had difficulty in keeping the image within the frame. We judged the wing span to be nearly two metres.

I climbed the cliff at one side of the nest site and sat on a safe ledge to secure some footage of a food pass. After a long wait it happened almost level with my perch. This time I had recorded the whole sequence and was elated. I stayed on the ledge to insert a new roll of film when to my horror the exposed reel slipped from my cold fingers. I held the loose end and watched, as in a nightmare, the film unwind in slow motion to its full length of a hundred feet. There went my best reel of film totally spoiled. One is not given a second chance.

The sky had turned a sullen grey with cumulus clouds building up like battleships; 'wind-ships' they are named in Icelandic myths, 'hope-of-showers' and 'drizzle-hope'. But we were hoping for sunshine.

Back in camp George prepared a meal with his usual speed and efficiency. He would not claim to be a cordon bleu but I doubt if anyone could beat him in speed. He delivered a bowl of hot soup into our hands by the time we had stripped off our wet clothes. Another of his specialities was dehydrated potatoes metamorphosised into a tasty dish of potato mash in a matter of seconds. Hunger is truly a good sauce.

We missed our daily hot bath enjoyed at Myvatn. I decided one morning to sharpen the edge of my considerable breakfast appetite by a swim in the stream that ran a few metres from our tent. It proved to be little more than one metre in depth but I did not prolong my immersion once I had stood up, for it was unbelievably cold. 'Runs over jagged rocks the river "Gruesome",' says the Elder Edda. I decided that this milk water from a nearby glacier must be that same river. My leap out was faster than my dive in. George and Harvey were prepared to take my word for it without personal verification.

Whilst we waited for the sun to illuminate the cliff, we scoured the fells with our glasses for any sign of Ptarmigan. There was none. In some years they have been as plentiful as Red Grouse on an English moor in the first week of August. We wondered at the cyclic rise and fall in numbers in a ten-yearly rhythm and, even more curiously, how the Gyrfalcon can anticipate the famine of game birds to adjust its family planning to suit the food supply.

But we did think it sad that our lordly hunter could not expend his strength and speed on some more worthy quarry than the gentle Redwing.

Harvey asked where the initial 'P' had come from as he knew the Gaelic name *tarmachan*, meaning 'inhabitant of high places'. I had made some research into this before we left England. The Gaelic name was anglicised into termigant in the early seventeenth century but was written in Sibbald's *Scotia Illustrata* as Ptarmigan, there being no better excuse for the initial 'P' than that it made the name appear to have a classical origin. 'In the ancient Celtic spoken throughout the British Isles before the Roman occupation, some words with an initial consonant were preceded with a P or Q. These represented a sound which cannot usually be pronounced by anyone speaking English.'

When we reached the hides the falcon was not standing by the nest in her customary guardian position but perched like a sentinel on a jutting rock at the very top of the cliff. She had puffed up her feathers as insulation against the chill wind. In the bright sunlight her breast was a more brilliant white than we had seen it and beautifully marked. The wind ruffled the feathers. She turned her proud head to left and right searching for a distant view of her life partner.

I shot a whole reel of film on her while she surveyed her domain, knowing I would never see so fine a sight again. Silhouetted against a background of scudding wisps of cloud across a cobalt sky and a foreground of granite boulders and wind-tossed ling, she was the essence of freedom, the epitome of power.

The pair bond in these falcons is very strong; they probably mate for life. I murmured a prayer for the siblings sleeping in the nest beneath her that they might be safely reared and launched into those wide ethereal garths which are their home. Standing fiercely on guard, she would let no predator do them harm. Only man, the arch-predator, might steal the chicks to sell for a great price in the world falconry market. We learned later that they were safely reared and flew strongly.

We left this most northerly of falcons, our long search ended. Rivalling the eagle in power and surpassing it in speed, its superb image is etched indelibly upon our minds, proudest of predators, fiercest of falcons.

Falcon food pass

CHAPTER TWO

The Isles of the Trinity

One lady whom I informed of my intention to visit Trinidad responded 'Oh, bad luck!' It is not the most favoured tourist island because of its oil industry, unobtrusive though that is, and because much of its shoreline is mangrove swamp.

My friend, George, and I had two very good reasons to watch and film birds in Trinidad, the Scarlet Ibis and the rare Oilbird. My wife decided to come with us for one reason only: the beautiful holiday island of Tobago is a short flight from Trinidad and it has wonderful beaches.

The island of Trinidad, named by Columbus for its three prominent hills, lies 10° north of the Equator. It is hot and humid, a paradise for bird watchers but hell for those whom insects love to bite. Such a one is my wife; if she exposed so much as a square inch of skin, she was attacked immediately and reacted with alarming swellings despite anti-histamines, insecticides and mollifying unguents. Life for her in Trinidad was only tolerable on the verandah protected by fly screens. This commanded a panoramic view of the whole Arina valley and overlooked a garden filled with flowering bushes, thus providing excellent birdwatching without suffering.

George and I are happily immune to insect poisons. They found our blood and skin little to their liking. Vast areas of bare skin on our legs and arms turned red and then brown without suffering attack. All very unfair! But life never has been fair and we have no reason to expect it to be so.

We had an introduction to a local bird enthusiast to make up our usual trio, one Jogi, who proved to be a treasure above price, knowledgeable, patient, and efficient.

I am surprised and deeply thankful that Trinidad is not yet overrun by ornithologists and entomologists. 420 distinct bird species have been recorded in the two islands of Trinidad and

Swallow-tailed Kite

Tobago, and over 600 species of butterfly. 127 of the bird species are winter migrants from the north but the rest breed there. There is no particular time of year for rearing young; breeding more often than once in twelve months the frequency and clutch size is influenced by rainfall and hence food supply. May, June and July are the peak breeding months but every month provides good bird watching.

The birds we found in Trinidad are more akin to the mainland birds of South America than to the oceanic birds of the Caribbean islands. The nearest tip of Trinidad is only sixteen kilometres from the coast of Venezuela and several tiny islands and rocks provide stepping stones between. Geographers say that the island was only separated from the mainland 1,200 years ago; birds have long inherited memories! The northern mountain range rising to 1,000 metres, is an eastward extension of the Venezuelan coastal Cordillera.

Although the island is small – ninety-seven kilometres north to south and sixty-eight kilometres east to west – it offers a great diversity of habitat: rainforest, swamps, savanna, cultivated fields and palm groves. This variety and the differing rainfall in each account for the unusually larger number of species in so small an area. We saw and identified 130 species in three hectic weeks and shot film of most of them. We would have been happy to stay for as many years because there were twice as many yet to see.

Very few of these bird species are the same as we see in Europe as are the Cattle Egret and the Osprey, or very similar to them, such as the Swallow and the Lapwing. Other species are recognisable as members of familiar genera, such as Woodpeckers, Orioles and Kingfishers. But the majority was entirely new to us; even their English names were very strange, such as Tinamou, Jacana, Motmot and Trogon. We soon mastered the names and became familiar with the appearance and habits of those we saw and were able to identify with Jogi's expert help.

After spending two nights in a luxury hotel in Port of Spain, we elected to live in quarters more suited to birdwatchers, the Asa Wright Nature Centre. After the noise and hustle of the crowded capital city it was a great delight to enjoy the tranquillity of this naturalists' guesthouse perched high above the Arina Valley in the densely wooded Northern Hills.

The Springfield Estate, in which the Nature Centre is located, used to produce coffee, cocoa and citrus fruits on a commercial scale but for many years it has been preserved only as a Nature Reserve, in which all wildlife is fully protected.

A preponderance of visitors comes from U.S.A. and Canada. All are keen naturalists, professional or amateur, and most were ornithologists when we were there. Breakfast was taken on the wide verandah protected on the three open sides by wire fly screens. There was scarcely sufficient space on the tables for crockery and cutlery because every guest had his or her binocular firmly planted on the table ready for instant seizure if any unusual bird should appear.

The Americans were tremendously keen. One young man, who was rarely seen without his field glasses raised to his eyes, replied to my comment, 'When I am birding, I certainly do watch birds!' Another, a professional scientist, walked the forest paths regularly three times a day, recording the numbers of each different bird species he saw or heard. He was researching for a census of bird population.

The view from the balcony is superb. One looks over the vivid green canopy of forest trees in the Arina Valley, falling steeply to the plains. Here and there the tallest trees break through this canopy towering to a height of forty metres, the immortelle, bright with scarlet blossom and the poui with vivid pink or yellow flowers. Within the estate is a profusion of citrus trees in bloom but no longer cultivated or harvested; also many coffee trees briefly decked with a lovely white blossom, to be followed all too soon by the small berries. There are cocoa trees too hung at that time with bright red pods. Banana trees abound which provide food for many birds; and there is a variety of palms. Blue in the distance rise the three mountains which give the island its name. What was once a well tended estate is now a wilderness of shrubs and trees, making a riot of colour and a perfumery of scents. Here we watched humming birds, brilliant in their iridescent plumage,

Humming Birds

drinking nectar from exotic blossoms.

They hover as if suspended, their wings invisible as they rotate up to eighty strokes a second, causing the humming sound for which they are well named. There were bees, competing for the same food source, almost as big as the smallest humming bird and producing a similar sound. There are seventeen different species of humming bird in the two islands; we saw and identified only seven of them.

As they dart from flower to flower they flash like the jewels which have given to several of them their specific names – ruby, emerald, topaz and sapphire. Only three metres from the main entrance to the Centre was the delicate nest of a Copper-rumped Hermit, a tiny humming bird weighing a mere five grammes. The suspended nest made of spiders' webs and the down of plants seemed too fragile to support the two nestlings. The hen bird fed them every few minutes with nectar and minute insects, hovering at the side entrance to the nest which could never have sustained her weight.

I believe these very slender and suspended nests are so designed that the erosion of time and weather reduces the strength of the structure and its suspension is inversely proportionate to the increasing weight of the nestling occupants so that the nest breaks up exactly when the fledglings are ready to fly. The fledglings would not otherwise be able to emerge from the small side exit, through which they have been fed by the parent.

The cock bird sang defiantly at regular intervals on his nearby perch to announce to all the world his territory which he would defend heroically against all comers whatever their size.

Another nest in a creeper up the wall of the house we watched being built by both parents; it was that of the Bananaquit, one of the tamest of birds which can be seen on most of the islands of the Caribbean. The nest is domed with a side entrance and it contained two eggs before we left; the cock starts the building to attract the hen and they finish it together. This very familiar bird will come onto a verandah or into a room to take sugar from a bowl on the table.

Honey creeper

From the high branches of a glorious immortelle tree a few metres down the road swung the strange nests of the Crested Oropendola. This large black bird with a brilliant yellow tail builds colonially its pendulant nest which may be two metres in length. It takes two to three weeks to build it with banana leaves, palm fibre and grass, starting with an entrance at the top and finishing with the bulbous egg chamber at the bottom. Though obvious for every predator to see, this species has a high breeding success because it is virtually impossible to reach the nests.

Perched on tree tops level with the verandah we often watched the Great Kiskadee calling out its own name. Many birds' local names are in French as a result of the one-time French occupation of the island; they thought this bird called '*qu'est ce qu'il dit*' and so named it. Each morning we put out some fruit on a bird-feeding table which was eagerly taken by a variety of Tanagers – the Blue-gray, the Palm and the Silver-beaked – and by the beautiful Honey-creepers and the well named Cocoa Thrush. This bird has a very musical song akin to our Song Thrush.

One of the most wonderful sights to be seen in the rain forest is the lek of the White-bearded Manakin. We were fortunate to be shown such a traditional display within the grounds of the estate where the male birds, at any time of day, may perform their fascinating dance. This site under the heavy growth of tropical trees and bushes was too dark to film but we took many still photographs in proximity. Provided we kept absolutely silent and quite still six or eight cock birds soon gathered and began their dance. They had cleared the forest floor of all the vegetable litter within an area of bare earth about a metre square. The first arrival picked up and carried away any odd leaf or twig which had fallen during their absence. When a few birds had assembled the displays began, even though no hen birds might be present.

The White-bearded Manakin cock is a most attractive little bird, about the size of a Great Tit but stouter, its crown, tail and wings black and the rest of the head and body a vivid white. It displays on a twig low to the ground by fanning its wings and then suddenly leaps like a firecracker onto another twig or to the ground with a loud snap, which sounds exactly like a stick being broken. This combination of leap-and-snap occurs every few seconds but with no regularity or pattern of movement. The effect is that of a number of firecrackers going off at random, sometimes in sequence and sometimes interrupted by the rapid fanning of wings or sliding down a stem. His call is a buzzing sound repeated at intervals.

Throughout the day we could hear at the Asa Wright Centre the clear ringing call of the Bearded Bellbirds. Perched on the topmost branch of a tall tree the grey and white cock bird with a brown head utters a loud single note repeated several times. This did not sound to me at all like a bell but exactly like a blacksmith striking a piece of metal on his anvil. This is a statement of territory which is answered by other Bellbirds on tree tops two hundred metres away. The 'beard' consists of a number of stringy black wattles hanging below a naked throat, which may be pushed out in a mating display.

We devoted two whole days to the Caroni Swamp yet this was not nearly a sufficient time. We engaged the services of a boat-owner named Winston Nanan, an Indian with an excellent knowledge of the swamp and its inhabitants. His steel boat fitted with an outboard engine was large enough for the three of us to move about easily with our encumbrance of cameras and binoculars and to set up tripods as required. We had no need of hides; Winston's technique was to motor through the narrow channels between the stilt-rooted mangrove trees and to shut off the engine as we entered each of the wide lagoons. Thus we approached quite close to a great variety of feeding birds with every chance to make excellent pictures.

The swamp is a nature reserve covering 10,000 hectares of salt and fresh water lagoons divided by mangrove forest and connected by narrow channels. The salt water area is tidal with a rise and fall of 1.22 metres, which at low tide exposes mudbanks, providing a valuable food supply to waders and waterfowl.

The Scarlet Ibis feeds during the breeding season in the freshwater swamps around the perimeter, filled with reeds and sedges, but at the time of our visit they were feeding at low tide on the mudflats and amongst the mangrove roots, whence they fly in

Scarlet Ibis

toward sunset to roost in the mangrove forest and especially on trees on selected islands. It is this spectacle of several hundreds of these great birds in their vivid scarlet plumage against a background of bright green trees which is the great tourist attraction. Unfortunately, we failed to see it. We waited until dusk and there was insufficient light to film, by which time we had been sitting for twelve hours on the hard steel seats in burning sun and could take no more. Winston, too, had very obviously had enough and wanted his cup of tea. So we missed the great tourist attraction but we did not miss the Ibis!

Earlier in the evening we had many splendid views of smaller flocks in tens, twenties or fifties circling above the tree tops and descending to roost with much noise of squeaky twittering. During the day we often saw single birds or small groups wading in the shallows or stalking through the mudflats probing for food with their long and slender curved bills. The groups often included immature birds in pale pink or grey plumage which do not achieve their glorious scarlet colour with black tips to the primary feathers until a year old.

The Scarlet Ibis is the national bird or Trinidad and appears on its postage stamps; it is now wholly protected. The population in the Caroni alone is estimated to be around six thousand.

As the tide was rising but the mudflats were not yet covered the fiddler crabs, evka, emerged from their holes in the mud. There are two species in the Caroni, the larger being the more numerous. It is a main item of diet for the Ibis and so they kept close to their holes whilst they waved the one great claw back and forth to catch anything edible which the tide might bring within reach. The visual effect is that of many Boy Scouts signalling to each other in semaphore in a rather desultory fashion.

Another curious sight of the Caroni is the 'four-eyed' fish with marks on the head which look exactly like two extra eyes. It measures about ten centimetres and is quite easily seen as it leaps out of the water to skim along the surface. We failed to catch sight of the Roseate Spoonbill which is an occasional summer visitor from the Americas and now extremely rare. This was really the only disappointment we had and Winston tried very hard to find one for us to see.

We filmed Great Egrets which are solitary feeders but communal roosters and do not breed in Trinidad. They stalked through the mud and shallows but were rather shy and tended to fly off as our boat approached. We were more fortunate with the Snowy Egret as we found a breeding colony of these elegant birds which are no longer common in the swamp. Their flimsy nests of sticks were closely packed on low bushes on an island. As we approached in absolute silence with the engine cut we were startled by the firing close at hand of two shots. It appeared that the unseen marksmen were firing at Cormorants roosting on the island nearby. The Egrets were even more startled and rose in a cloud with hoarse cries from the nests. When they at last re-settled we secured some excellent film shots. The target of the shooters would be the Neotropic Cormorant and I cannot suppose it would make good eating.

In another lagoon we approached the shore to examine the suspended nest of the White-headed Marsh Tyrant. This is a common resident bird which builds a domed nest hanging over the water to protect the eggs from predatory snakes.

It was as the engine was re-started and engaged that we had the misfortune to shear a pin in the transmission to the propeller. As we were several miles distant from dry land the situation looked serious with the daylight being already far spent. However, Winston did not appear too concerned. He cut a twig from an overhanging tree and proceeded to fashion a wooden pin. When fitted this also failed but happily another boat came into view. The Indian occupants came to our rescue; although they had no engine spares they quickly extracted a nail from their wooden freeboard which was cut to size and fitted to the universal coupling. It took us safely home and may well be still functioning!

We were lucky to see another visitor from the north, the Lesser Yellowlegs, which breeds within the Arctic Circle and had travelled a long way to feed on small crustacea along this tropical tide-line. We saw three other species of heron in the course of two long days in the Caroni – the Little Blue, the Streaked, and the Yellow-crowned Night Heron. We watched

Snowy Egret

also the Little Egret so that our knowledge of the family Ardeidae was greatly increased and our time in the Caroni well spent. It is being drained at rather an alarming rate but hopefully sufficient wetland will remain to provide sanctuary to this wonderful reservoir of marsh birds.

We ascended by car the winding road to the summit of the Northern Range at 600 metres and then down to sea level where lies the village of Blanchisseuse on the northern coast. Why it is named 'the washerwoman' we never learned. We stopped very frequently either because we had been told in advance what birds we might expect to see in particular places or because Jogi's sharp eyes had spotted a new bird. One of these was the Channel-billed Toucan which frequents the canopy of tall forest trees and is difficult to see but easy to hear. It repeats its loud high-pitched single note at short intervals and we all had a crick in the neck by the time we had located it among the dense foliage. It is a big bird and, of course its bill is unmistakable, being disproportionately large. Through glasses we could admire its bright colours: the bill black with a blue base, forehead light blue, chin and throat white, breast red and orange, and the rest black except for the red upper tail-coverts. But we were unable to secure any good film of it. This bird nests in deep holes in hollow trees but I was told it does not plaster up the entrance hole as do other species of Toucan which I have watched elsewhere. These plaster the entrance with clay when the hen has laid her clutch so that she is imprisoned until the young are hatched and fledged. The cock bird feeds her and later the two young through the diminished hole which she has closed as a protection from snakes. In the early stages of the incubation he is very smart and alert but by the time his family emerges he is 'on his knees' and quite bedraggled.

Jogi was expert in imitating the call of the Tropical Kingbird which is a grey bird with brilliant yellow breast found in both islands. When he imitated its single high note and trill one soon answered him and kept calling as it came progressively nearer until we had an excellent view of it and took some good film shots.

I deprecate the use of sound recordings on tape to call in any bird species as I feel sure that it must confuse a bird to hear the unmistakable call of its own species, whether it be a potential mate or an intruder into its territory, and to find none there: any action which causes distress to a wild creature is to be avoided. Quite illogically I am prepared to condone imitation by the human voice. I assume this is because it involves skill and practice and the result is still likely to be imperfect so that the bird only comes if its curiosity overcomes its natural caution. Anyhow, Jogi could imitate the call of many species and I made use of his skill.

He took us on foot through thick jungle to another dancing floor of the White-bearded Manakin but, although we waited for quite a while, there was no dancing that day. Probably the time was wrong. But we did see a beautiful Violaceous Trogon perched on a forest tree and calling like a flautist; the male and female look very similar and this might have been either – dark blue or violet except for the belly which is bright yellow and the black tail barred with horizontal white stripes.

Blanchisseuse is a scattered village of houses and chapels constructed for the most part of corrugated iron and straggling along the sea-front. Beyond it the road leads through coconut palm groves. The sea was rough and the wind boisterous. Big waves thundered on the rocks or raced up the sand beach. Sea birds familiar to us were flying offshore – the Brown Pelican fishing with its clumsy dive, the Magnificent Frigate Bird soaring so easily on its vast wing span, and the Red-billed Tropic Bird with its direct and purposeful flight, trailing a long white tail.

We searched along the banks of the insignificant River Damia, which flows into the sea to the east of Blanchisseuse, for the Pygmy Kingfisher which is one of the several members of that family which none of us had hitherto seen. At last we had a glimpse of one perched in a bush above the water but, alas, too brief to expose any film. It is very small and coloured much like our European species but perhaps not so vivid and having white spots on the wings.

No less than ninety living species of the Kingfisher family are recorded and these are well spread throughout the world. They include the Laughing and the Blue-winged Kookaburras of Australia, and all are clearly recognisable as Kingfishers with a

powerful dagger bill and brilliant plumage. The bright colours
vary between species, as also does the size from the Giant
Kingfisher of Africa measuring forty-six centimetres in length to
the tiny Pygmy Kingfisher measuring fourteen centimetres.

The family name Alcedinidae is derived from the Greek name
for the Kingfisher *halkyon* from *hals* meaning 'the sea' and *kyon*
meaning 'conceiving'.

Our word 'halcyon' comes from the same source due to a
delightful Greek legend that the Kingfisher incubates its eggs on a
nest which floated on the sea and the gods provided two weeks of
calm weather before the winter solstice so that they could hatch
their eggs in safety.

The ancient Greek naturalists were romantic! In their
mythology Halkyon was one of the daughters of Atlas and one of
the seven Pleiades. When her lover, Poseidon, was drowned,
she threw herself into the sea; the gods took pity on her and
turned them both into birds.

The forest species have been given the Latin name of *Dacelo*,
which is merely an anagram of Alcedo, showing a singular lack of
imagination in our modern taxonomists.

There were groves of coconut palms between the beach and the
road where Mocking Birds were flying; high overhead we saw our
first Swallow-tailed Kite.

Jogi took us to his home to show us some of the birds in its
capacious grounds. It was rather a splendid house of wood with a
wide verandah. David Snow had lived there for six years and
Richard French had also stayed there, so it had a reputation of
being a good base for bird watching. He wished especially to show
us the nest of a Blue-chinned Sapphire Humming Bird by the side
of a path. A photographer had been taking pictures of it on the
previous day. Alas, he had been too persistent and too close: the
birds had deserted the nest. Jogi was very sad. A piece of cloth
left attached to a bush on the other side of the path only a metre
away from the nest had obviously been placed by him for a hide.
Although humming birds are usually tolerant of human presence,
this had proved too much. The nest was tiny, the size of a cotton
reel, and beautifully made of plant down. At the bottom

of the deep cup lay two oval eggs, white with brown spots and now quite cold.

A flock of about a hundred parrots flew high above us, calling in flight. They are noisy birds. They were Blue-headed Parrots which spend most of their lives among the high tops of giant trees and occasionally scream to others across the valley. Parrakeets and Macaws also abound.

Two Bearded Bellbirds were calling at each other within this wonderful garden but a new and exciting bird we saw there was the Striped Cuckoo, which is smaller than the other six cuckoos found here. It has the characteristic long tail but does not call 'cuckoo' at all; instead it has a musical whistle. Like the Cuckoo which breeds in Britain, it is parasitic, laying one or two eggs in the nest of Spinetails, whose own young are probably ejected from the nest built close to the ground. This reminded us that not all Cuckoos are parasitic, nor is the Cuckoo the only species that is.

The loveliest bird we saw there was the Blue-crowned Motmot, also named Swainson's Motmot and 'King of the Woods', or in the local patois 'bouhoutou' because of its call. One partner calls 'bou' and the other replies 'hou' but I do not know which. So do our Tawny Owls at home call 'tuwhit' and are answered 'tuwhu'. This large and beautiful bird has a peculiar racquet-shaped tail which it swings from side to side like a pendulum as it roosts on a horizontal branch. It digs a deep tunnel in an earth bank for its nest. We did not find the nest but we obtained some fine shots with the film camera before it flew away.

We made a special trip up to Aripo Valley to El Naranjo Estate whose owner had made special arrangements to attract humming birds. Around an open-fronted verandah on the first floor they had hung several vessels which dripped a sugar solution. We watched the Blue-headed Sapphire, the Black-throated Mango, the Brown Violetear and three other species of humming bird not clearly identified. All these we saw while merely sitting at ease in cane chairs sipping cool drinks. But our photography was not so good as the birds moved with such speed and drank the nectar for too short a time at each station.

On our return journey a whipsnake crossed the road and our driver swerved to run over it but happiiy did not succeed. In our brief glimpse of it we judged it to be nearly one and a half metres in length and no thicker than one's finger.

We spent another day watching the birds of the savanna, chiefly in the neighbourhood of the agricultural station which is a Government enterprise designed to improve the quality of cattle. As we might have expected, the first birds we saw there were Cattle Egrets, which have now spread from Africa throughout all warm climates of the world. But it scarcely competes with other egrets for food because it has found a rewarding food source in the insect life stirred up by the feet of grazing cattle and this is where they may be always seen.

The Red-breasted Blackbird describes very exactly the next bird we filmed without any hide as it fed on beetles on the ground. Locally it is named the Trinidad Robin although it bears no relation to our European Redbreast. Throughout the English speaking world any small bird with a red breast may be called a Robin, which just confirms the popularity of our friendly garden companion – *Erithacus rubecula*. It used to be named in English the Redbreast and the pre-name Robin was just an affectionate pet-name such as we have in English for several of the most common birds: such as Jackdaw, Tom-tit, Magpie and so on. Actually our Robin's breast is coloured orange rather than red, or to be more precise, it is rust. Another bird in Trinidad is locally named Robin; it is the Bare-eyed Thrush which has no red on its breast at all but looks like a thrush and so it is. So you may call a bird what you wish and the only accurate name which is understood by ornithologists world-wide is the scientific name. But even this can change in time if taxonomists decide one has been placed in the wrong family!

The breast of the bird we were filming was unequivocally red. Its courting display was a high-pitched song in flight, followed by a sudden dive to the ground with wings folded. It was an easy bird to film without a hide and we were obliged to it.

We saw two new hawks that day, one was the Savanna Hawk which is red-brown in colour, mottled above and barred below, with a black tail. It sat on a post watching for lizards but we did not see it catch any. The other was the Common Black Hawk.

The station was divided by single strands of barbed wire into small 'camps' to graze cattle; the bulls were Brahmin and the cows Friesian. In one of the camps was a small pond with several very familiar birds flying around it or resting on the banks; they were Lapwings, not our European bird but the Southern Lapwing, which is a distinct species, very like our own in appearance and behaviour.

We had to call at a village police station to film a colourful and gregarious bird, the Yellow-rumped Cacique. A tall tree grows in front of the main door and we thought it prudent to obtain permission to avoid spending a night in the cells. This was readily given and we set up our tripods at a distance and slowly advanced them nearer. There must have been nearly a hundred suspended nests in the colony and the birds were much too busy flying in and out of them to bother about us. The nest hangs down about fifty centimetres with an entrance at one side close to the top. It is built by the hen of plant fibres and lined with vegetable down.

She incubates the eggs and feeds the young without any help from her mate, who sings very melodiously with a series of liquid notes, and engages in an interesting courtship display before any unattached hen with much bowing of the head and fluttering of the wings. The hens out-number the cocks in any colony and the cocks are polygamous and relieved of all parental duties. Perhaps because of this loose family structure the Giant Cowbird lays its eggs in the nest of this species, but we did not discern whether the young Cowbird ejects the eggs or young of the Cacique. This is yet another species of the widespread American Oriole family; it is sometimes named the Yellow Oriole and there is another Cacique in Trinidad called the Smaller Cacique which is actually larger than the bird we filmed.

We went on to the Elsecoro Swamp which is choked with vegetation so we explored it on foot. We were rewarded by good sightings of the Wattled Jacana which were present in fair numbers, including many delightful young, which are feathered very differently from their parents. They are members of the

Yellow-rumped Cacique

Lilytrotter family with long legs and excessively long toes to spread their weight; this enables them to walk delicately over floating vegetation. Each wing has a sharp spur at the wrist, which is presumably used by the males in conflict and defence; he does all the incubation and takes care of the precocial young.

We were intent on watching Giant Cowbirds beside another pond, when we observed two eyes just above the surface of the pond watching us with equal interest. We saw it was quite a large alligator which had travelled overland from the swamp. As these animals have been known to make a rush out of the water to snatch a meal and this specimen was taking a very keen interest in us, there being not much to eat in that small pond, we took a quick film shot and retreated to a safer distance.

Our next stop was at the home of Dr Richard French who wrote the text of that excellent and informative book *A Guide to the Birds of Trinidad and Tobago*. He and his wife Margaret received us very graciously on the verandah of their charming home within the Texaco compound at Point a Pierre. His knowledge of the birds of these two islands is encyclopaedic and he solved many of our identification problems for us. We met their daughter Lintie, appropriately christened Linnet as the daughter of an ornithologist.

After welcome cool drinks, Richard directed us to his 'Wildfowl Trust' where we could see some rare and endangered species whilst he fulfilled his teaching commitments, for he is a schoolmaster. The White-necked Heron does not breed in Trinidad but is a regular visitor to fish in the fresh-water lakes. We found this stately black, grey and white bird standing immobile and enjoying its solitude. There was no problem in taking as many photographs as we wished as it looked down its black dagger bill with the yellow tip pointed at the water.

The Black-bellied Tree-duck was also there, protected from ruthless hunters. Once very common in Trinidad, it was hunted almost to extinction both for food and for the damage it did to the rice fields. Now it is a protected species and hopefully its numbers will recover. But it is not easy to enforce this law and the duck doubtless makes good eating. So we were pleased to find a

Black-bellied
Tree Duck

nucleus of this colourful species protected in the reserve. We saw the Boat-tail here which manoeuvres its long tail like the rudder of a boat. The early French occupants of Trinidad named it *'Merles a Queue au Bateau'* so they evidently had the same idea.

On our drive home three ominous birds sat on a fence by the roadside waiting for a vehicle to hit some creature so as to provide their next meal. They were Turkey Vultures, which have the usual sombre colouring of vultures but lightened by bare red heads and necks. It feeds on carrion which it sees at a great distance as it soars effortlessly on its two metre span wings tilted vertically. They flapped off when we stopped to film them.

Twice we visited the Gaucharo caves with a guide from the Nature Centre. These are the breeding place of the Oilbird, one of the two avian species we had come to Trinidad especially to see. On the first visit we came to look only and on the second visit we came suitably equipped to photograph and to film. We were not disappointed.

This strange bird is the single species in its family Steatornithidae; it is found mainly in Trinidad, with a few in Venezuela, Columbia, Peru, Bolivia and Panama; it is nocturnal; it breeds in caves in mountainous country where the site is usually inaccessible.

It is a big bird with a one metre wing span and is half a metre in length with a hooked bill and short legs. It looks somewhat like a big Nightjar but differs in many ways from that species. In colour it is overall a rich brown with numerous white spots on the wing coverts and secondary feathers. The tail is horizontally barred with darker brown.

There are eight colonies in Trinidad; five more have recently died out and those remaining are strongly protected.

We were led into a deep and steep-sided gulley situated close to the Nature Centre. The cave was a fissure in the rock, only partially closed at the top but nevertheless very dark. A stream emerged from it so that we were obliged to jump from rock to rock. As we penetrated deeply we heard the strange noises made by these birds resenting our intrusion. They made no attempt to

* Its correct English name is Carib Grackle.

fly out of the exit but emitted snarls and screams which must have frightened many an intruder.

The nests are mounds of regurgitated fruit, either built on ledges or stuck to the rock walls, and having a slight depression in which are laid two or three white eggs. The young remain in the nest for twelve or more weeks during which time they grow very fat on their diet of oil nuts. This is their misfortune because they were collected at the peak of their obesity by the early inhabitants of these countries and rendered down to provide oil for cooking or lamps.

Both parents feed them. The whole colony emerges after dark to feed on palm nuts and other fruit which they swallow whole and regurgitate to feed the young. They probably locate the food source by the sense of smell but within the darkness of the breeding site they locate by sonar like bats.

The fissure in the rock widened into a cave, closed at the top but with a small opening at the farther end. Our lamps revealed many nests clinging to the sides or standing on ledges. As it was day time these were all occupied by incubating parents with other adults crouching by the nests. The air was filled with the noise of grunts and growls. In flight they emit a click, which provides the sonar echo but only one or two birds flew from end to end of the cave and none went out of it. We stayed for only a few minutes to avoid disturbance.

We returned on another day with cameras and flash. Knowing what to expect, we entered circumspectly and caused no disturbance. We were able to take many still photographs and some film which did not come out well. But the stills were satisfactory with the flash reflected from the eyes of the sitting birds. Undoubtedly both male and female birds were there but we could not distinguish between them. We counted twenty-two breeding pairs. I was pleased that this colony is increasing in size and this rare and intensely interesting species is no longer in danger of extinction.

We made the short plane hop from Trinidad to Tobago in the evening of March 12th, where a short car journey took us to the Arna Vale Hotel. Once installed with balconies overlooking the glorious beach and the blue ocean, it required great resolution on the part of George and myself not to spend the whole week sunbathing on the golden sand and swimming in the clear warm water. But there is so much to see of wildlife and human history that we managed to drag ourselves away from these sensuous pleasures.

Tobago's economy was based on the production of sugar and rum until the end of the last century but now it is devoted to tourism with a choice of several fine hotels. Only a huge rusting iron water wheel, which once provided power for a sugar mill, reminded us of the earlier prosperity. It is a beautiful island in spite of the hurricane which devastated so much of its natural forest in 1963. At the coast many royal and coconut palms have survived and elsewhere the vegetation is recovering.

People in Tobago claim that this is Robinson Crusoe's island and Defoe's tale seems to support this. But Alexander Selkirk may have been marooned on an island in the Pacific – perhaps in the Galapagos archipelago. Had it been Tobago, he would have been foolish ever to have left it for there is no more idyllic place on earth. There is nearby a small island named Little Tobago which can be reached by motor-boat from Speyside. It was here that an attempt was made in 1929 to establish the Greater Bird of Paradise from New Guinea, where it was in grave danger of extinction because of the demand by the European millinery trade for its lovely plumage. The number of birds surviving on Little Tobago has gradually diminished and there are now few pairs left. We climbed from the landing stage up the forest path to reach an observation hut in the early evening when any surviving birds would come to roost in the high tree canopy. After a long wait we were fortunate to catch a fleeting glimpse of a solitary cock. Was this the sole survivor of a bold experiment? I believe not quite, but chances of survival of the colony are slight.

On the way up we had stopped to watch many Red-billed Tropic Birds flying to and from their breeding places on ledges on a great cliff face. Their long white tails made them very graceful in flight. They alone would have made the short sea trip to Little Tobago worthwhile.

From a deck chair on the hotel beach we could watch Magnificent Frigate Birds sailing past, Brown Pelicans tumbling into the ocean, and Brown Boobies plunging in with a more elegant dive. Sanderlings and Turnstones ran along the tideline. Among the palm trees we watched Mocking Birds and Ruddy Ground Doves scratching among the fallen fronds.

We hired a car, the driver of which solemnly assured us his christened name was 'Sir Walter Raleigh' and thus we addressed him. Encouraged by this courtesy he took us to a forest area in the mountain range, which we might not otherwise have found; there he claimed we would be sure to see the rare Blue-backed Manakin; but we did not. However, we had a splendid view of the Red-crowned Woodpecker feeding young in a hole high up a bare tree trunk. This we filmed with a very satisfactory result. This species is common in Tobago but not found in Trinidad, which has seven other species of this family, none of which venture to cross the forty-two kilometres of ocean which divides the two islands. Its high-pitched rattling call became familiar to us and we often heard the rapid drumming of its powerful bill as it drove holes through the bark to extract insects with its long telescopic tongue.

Another forest bird we had come to see is the Rufous-vented Chachalaca. The name is onomatopoeic and the bird is endemic to Tobago. It has been adopted as the national emblem of Tobago and appears on the island's postage stamps. We went up the hill to the Grafton Estate to see it. This estate is owned by a Mrs Alefounder who took pity on these and other birds when the hurricane destroyed their breeding sites and food sources around her spacious house. She put out food for them each afternoon and has done so ever since. Now she generously shares her pleasure by allowing any visitors to climb the stone steps up to her wide balcony and to watch the birds when one of her staff sounds a gong and has put out the food. Then follows an astounding sight.

The Chachalaca is the largest bird in the two islands, as big as a small turkey, sixty centimetres long, which lives in forest trees: it is normally shy and very rare, because it was remorselessly hunted for food. It feeds on leaves, fruit and berries and it calls its name in the morning and evening twilight.

At the sound of the gong half a dozen of these astonishing birds came sidling down the tree branches or walking with prim steps along them to reach the bowls of meal set out on a plank level with the verandah. I noted its plumage was brown with a grey head and neck and a bare red throat.

There was a large green iguana static on the ground. It looked very dangerous but I was assured it is a harmless creature. It measured, as I judged, about two metres in length. Other birds come regularly at the sound of the gong, notably the Motmot, Barred Ant-shrike and the Scaly-breasted Ground-dove.

In a magnolia tree on the beach a hen humming bird, a White-chested Emerald was building a nest about two metres from the ground being quite unperturbed by the hotel guests walking to the beach. This tiny mite of a bird worked assiduously for hours on end in the early morning and in the evening, stopping only in the hottest part of the day. It seemed that the hen did the building alone and she came on average every two minutes with plant material to weave into the delicate structure.

The nest was a deep cup, the size of a reel of thread, standing on a slender branch and constructed of plant-fibre. She made one determined attempt to pluck a white hair from the head of an old lady who lay asleep in a deck chair on the beach, but gave up when she awoke. As each length of fibre was woven into the structure she pushed her breast against the inside wall and revolved within the nest to shape it; then she leaned out her head to shape the outside circumference with her long bill.

One bird, with which we became very familiar but never saw, was the Ferruginous Pygmy Owl. At sundown every evening it began its monotonous and repetitive double hoot which continued until dawn. At first it sounded delightfully musical and romantic, as it should be as it is a prelude to mating. But after a long day of bird watching we could have well done without it to enjoy a good night's sleep but that sound still haunts our dreams of these two lovely islands.

Ferruginous Pygmy-Owl

CHAPTER THREE

The Skeleton Coast

Between the cold Benguela Current sweeping north from the Antarctic and the fierce heat of the Namib Desert on the western edge of Namibia there lies the most dangerous coastline in the world, which has earned its name from the skeletons of ships and men. It is pounded by the great Atlantic rollers and often shrouded in fog due to the violent contrast of temperatures. The coastline varies with the shifting sands of the 'smoking dunes' and very occasionally heavy rain inland brings a flash flood down river beds that have been dry for years, pushing millions of tons of sand and debris into the sea.

This harsh coastline and the desert behind it is hostile to man and other predators but it provides a safe refuge for birds – the marine birds which are able to drink salt water, the few species of desert birds which can survive long periods and fly great distances without water, and the waders which come in their thousands from Europe and the far north to winter in the warm sunshine at the few places where fresh water may be found. Sometimes also one may see indigenous water birds which flock to the coast when drought dries up inland lakes and salt pans.

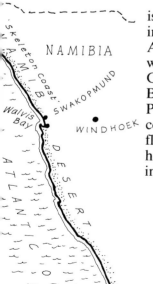

The Namib Desert, which has given the country its new name, is thought to be the oldest in the world and certainly it is the most inhospitable to life; it stretches for 1,000 kilometres from the Angolan border in the north to the Orange River in the south, with an average width of 130 kilometres, relieved only by the old German port of Swakopmund and the old British port of Walvis Bay. South of the latter has been established the Namib Desert Park for the scientific study of what little life can survive in these conditions of extreme aridity. We did see and film there a small flock of six Dune Larks feeding on the ground where they cannot have found more than a sparse scatter of wind-blown seeds or tiny insects. They were very active, fluttering close to the ground and never allowing us to approach. We found some wild melons growing on a sand dune, about the size of a small orange, among a tangle of surface roots which scarcely penetrated the sand. We wondered how they obtained any moisture or nutrient in such a location.

A little north of Swakopmund there is a large area of salt pans from which the water is evaporated to leave the salt for commercial purpose. Here we saw and filmed a few Flamingos, both the Greater and the Lesser, which had doubtless come from dried-up lakes inland. Because of the small size of the pans and their preference for those few with the desired degree of salinity, we were able to approach quite near to them without causing any alarm and were able to study the difference between the two species and between adults and juveniles in some detail. The Greater is, of course, larger but also its bill is more sharply curved, of which one third of the length is black and the rest is pink. The Lesser species has its bill less curved and all red, except for a black tip.

There was a large flock of Curlew Sandpipers of more than one hundred birds, which were busily probing the algae with their de-curved bills. This is a winter visitor from the high north of Europe and these tiny birds seemed oblivious to our presence due, perhaps, to hunger after a long flight over the desert. Marsh and Common Sandpipers were also feeding in singles and pairs; there were several Greenshank treading delicately over the surface of the ponds, their long legs and large feet supporting them without penetration of the surface crust, their long black bills probing continuously for insects or molluscs. There were gulls there too, the Lesser Black-backed, the Grey-headed, and Hartlaub's, which latter George and I had not seen before. It is smaller than the other two, white with a grey back and black wing tips; and the legs and bill are dark red in colour. Its habits are akin to those of our Herring Gull in England.

On the outskirts of Walvis Bay we visited an extensive sewage farm which rather resembled a series of small lakes with many islands and luxurious arboreal growth. The several species of fresh-water birds were very tame and evidently accustomed to

Curlew
Sandpipers

human visitors. The Great Crested Grebe, the Cape Dabchick and the Moor-hen are like our European species but the Purple Gallinule and the Red-knobbed Coot were new to George and myself. We had only brief glimpses of the former hidden amongst the vegetation on the banks but its large size, vivid blue colouring and bright red bill are unmistakable. The Coots, on the other hand, were almost too obvious; they sailed high in the water in groups of up to twenty, coming to the water's edge, being evidently accustomed to take food from visitors. They are all black with a white bill and frontal shield surmounted by two red knobs which in the adult birds are very conspicuous. There was a good variety of duck on the water and we had no difficulty in identifying the Whitefaced Tree Duck, the Maccoa Duck and three species of Teal – the Red-billed, the Cape, and the Hottentot. The blue bill and green speculum convinced us that this was the Hottentot Teal which we had not expected to find here. The Smith's Shoveller was identified by its broad and flattened bill but the drake lacked the bright colours of the European Shoveller; it was a dull brown, maybe in eclipse.

We had anticipated this site would be odiferous but it was not so; we made no haste to return to Walvis Bay which held little for us to see. The houses there are raised from ground level, due, I was told, to the prevalence of sand storms.

At some distance offshore, platforms had been built as artificial islands to encourage the roosting and nesting of the White Pelican and various species of Cormorant, the Pelicans and Cape Cormorants on the platform and the Crowned Cormorant on the beams and struts beneath it. The nearest of these had an overhead cable connected to the shore by which the harvest of guano could be landed. This was not in operation and it appeared that the harvesting of guano, for which the platforms had been erected, was finished by the end of February. But there were still many birds roosting on the platforms and on the two-legged supports for the cable, as well as others constantly coming and going. We watched these for some while and established that there were White-breasted or Great Cormorants with a greenish sheen on their black feathers akin to our Shag; the breast was

Marsh
Sandpipers

white from chin to belly and the legs black; no crest was visible. The Cape Cormorant was smaller with an orange gular pouch and the Bank Cormorant was unrelieved black in colour. The three species of Cormorants in total outnumbered the White Pelicans in the proportion of three to one. In the height of the breeding season these artificial islands are said to be thronged by hundreds of birds and their droppings cover the platforms with a thick layer of guano which provides a valuable harvest of nitrate fertiliser.

On the following day we set out on a sand buggy across the dunes to Sandvis, which used to be known as Sandwich Harbour, although there is no harbour there. This is a wonderful place for birds because fresh water from the Kuiseb River seeps through beneath the sand dunes of the Namib Desert to emerge into the Atlantic Ocean where it forms a brackish lagoon. There also are tidal mudflats, salt marshes, and a sandy shore at low tide, providing a variety of habitat and some green vegetation of reed, sedge and bulrush with coarse grasses. There are remains of wooden buildings once used by fishermen as temporary lodging but now completely deserted. The plethora of birds was amazing.

White Pelicans were rising in circles upon a thermal which lifted them with scarcely a wing beat to about a thousand feet. They made a lovely sight against the vivid blue sky. The air space from ground to the highest level was filled with more than a hundred of these stately birds sailing upwards in majestic circles, apparently without effort. Having reached the desired height, they would glide down to sea level perhaps forty miles along the coast to a fresh feeding ground. However, some twenty birds remained and later in the day, when the tide was ebbing, we witnessed the rare sight of communal fishing. As water drained from the tidal pools the fish were concentrated in shallow water; the pelicans formed a circle which closed in on the shoal; then followed a pandemonium of leaping fish and slashing beaks with gulls and terns flying and crying overhead. It was all over in two or three minutes with the fish safely pouched in the capacious lower mandibles of the pelicans.

Far out on the sandy sea shore were groups of terns – the Common, and Arctic which were not then distinguishable and the

Little Egret.

Sandwich with its black and yellow bill, all of which breed on the coasts and islands of Europe. There were three Caspian Terns outstanding by their much larger size and red bill, which do not breed on the coast of Namibia but do on the south and east coasts of South Africa. The small Damara Tern does breed here during the winter months. We believed that we saw amongst the ever-moving kaleidoscope of fluttering terns the Black Tern and the White-winged Tern, but we could not identify these with certainty.

We turned our attention to the brackish lagoon where we filmed the Little Egrets nesting in a colony amongst the vegetation on the shore of the lagoon. The nests were low down so we could easily film these slim and elegant birds sitting on their platform nests or stepping daintily from branch to branch. They are all white except for the slender black bill and black legs with yellow feet. The delicate and lovely white plumes drooping from the back of the head were the cause of the near extinction of this species when the aigrettes were much in demand by milliners. There were two Great White Egrets stalking slowly through the deeper water, which were nearly twice the size of the Little, and a solitary Grey Heron standing motionless in the shallows with its long yellow bill poised to strike.

A pair of Great Crested Grebes were performing their nuptial greeting ceremony near the centre of the lagoon. They were circling and bowing to each other with the crests erect in a charming and elegant quadrille. This is the identical species that we enjoy watching in U.K. and, indeed, throughout Europe except in the high north; it is not migratory but is resident in Cape Province and Natal. We were surprised to find it in so dry an area as Namibia.

It is almost impossible to resist filming the Avocet. There were a dozen of these beautiful black and white birds standing in shallow water and sweeping their long up-curved bills over the surface to collect insects. The little flock was continually re-grouping and in every position and every grouping they made a perfect picture. I know of no other bird which is so photogenic. These may have been local birds resident in South Africa or

Black-winged Stilt

migrants from the coasts of Europe where they also breed. Another long-legged bird was much more shy and could not be approached closely – the Black-winged Stilt. This inhabits the shores of lakes and estuaries throughout the world in warm countries; it is nomadic and not migratory. Its red legs are excessively long and it steps carefully through shallow water as it searches for food on the surface or beneath it. When disturbed it utters a shrill alarm call.

One of the most interesting sights was a large flock of Bar-tailed Godwits thrusting their heavy bills into the sand at the tide line. There were forty to fifty birds which we are accustomed to see solitary on our English shores on migration or in pairs breeding in the extreme north of Norway and Finland.

There was a Black Oystercatcher feeding alongside the other waders at the tide line. In shape and habits it looked identical to our familiar black and white Oystercatcher with its great orange-red bill and prominent red eye-ring but this bird was completely black instead of pied black and white. It utters the same loud piping call but is peculiar to Africa, whereas our European Oystercatcher rarely migrates so far south.

We saw a fine selection of Plovers – some familiar and some new to us: the Grey and the Ringed we know in Europe, but the White-fronted, the Three-banded and the Kittlitz's were new. The three black and white bands on the neck made that one easy to identify, as did the black and white markings on the head of Kittlitz's. We started our return journey in good time so as to reach Walvis Bay before dark. Some of the dunes rise to 300 metres and had to be negotiated with great care. The very low tyre pressures of our vehicle made it possible to cross areas of soft sand but even so we were sometimes in danger of sinking. It is then fatal to spin the wheels which would dig a grave in a few seconds. The correct procedure is to reverse gently along the track already made and then to explore on foot for harder ground. Should the vehicle be immobilised one must never set out to walk in daylight. The heat is so great and the aridity so severe that one would have small chance of survival. The only route to safety is to walk at night and, if one has no compass to steer a direct line, to follow the coast. To be lost in the Namib Desert would be certain death.

On our return journey by car to Swakopmund and thence to Outjo we were fortunate to have a good view of three other African birds – the Kori Bustard, the Black Korhaan, and the Secretary Bird. We saw the male Kori Bustard in the sandveld and drove off the road to approach it. He is a huge bird with a horizontal crest on the back of his grey head; his thick neck is also mottled grey and the belly is white; his back and wings are brown; he quickened his walking pace to maintain his distance from us but did not take flight. He was of a heavy build like a large turkey, very conspicuous on the veld and said to be rather rare.

The *Black Korhaan is not so rare, nor so large. We stopped the car to watch a male bird perform his display flight which is very spectacular. The hen was not visible but must have been present, hidden in the scrub. He flew to a height of ten or twelve metres calling loudly, hung for a few seconds with rapidly beating wings, and then descended slowly like a parachute with his yellow legs hanging down and his harsh croaks decreasing in volume. When he reached the ground he ran off into the scrub. His wings and back were mottled black and fawn, head, neck and belly black with white patches on the cheeks and neck.

We had two splendid views of the Secretary Bird which is very obvious as it stalks along on its excessively long legs searching for lizards and small mammals and, occasionally, for snakes. Its long crest of black feathers droops from the top of its head down the nape like quill pens behind the ear of a Dickensian clerk. The long tail and upper legs are black and the lower parts pink; the rest of the feathering is pale grey and the bare skin on the cheeks a vivid orange. It is beautiful and elegant with rather a fierce appearance and a haughty look. It seemed to be reluctant to fly and went only for twenty to thirty metres in the air before landing again to continue its striding gait.

On an isolated acacia tree some distance from the road we saw a hen bird standing upright on the very top. Our guide said it

* Or Little Black Bustard.

would be standing on its nest, which was invisible and we should take a closer look. As we drove off the road to approach the tree it sank out of sight and we could hardly believe it was still there. We stopped some ten metres away and could now see the flat nest hidden in the leafy crown but no sign of the bird. We stood on the roof of the car to obtain a photograph but as we straightened up the hen bird launched into the air with huge wings and flew off to land at a distance. There were chicks in the shallow nest crouched too low for us to see well.

The name of Secretary Bird is usually attributed to the drooping crest. If this were the origin of the vernacular English name, it should have been 'Clerk Bird' for our English Secretaries of State are not commonly seen with pens behind the ear; and our secretaries in commerce and industry are more likely to be seated at a computer or electric word-processor than using a pen. It has been suggested to me that the Arabic name for this bird, which can be literally translated as 'snake-bird' sounds very like the French word *secretoire* and was so adopted by the French colonists in the Middle East. This would naturally be translated by English-speaking ornithologists as Secretary Bird. Knowing the ability of this elegant bird to kill snakes, I find this a much more acceptable explanation of the name.

CHAPTER FOUR

The Island of Flowers

Madeira is sometimes named the Pearl of the Atlantic but I prefer another name – the Island of Flowers – for it is notable for its profusion of wild flowers in any month of the year. Species which are treasured in our gardens grow wild along the roadside or cover the lower slopes of the mountains. I visited it in February for the winter sunshine rather than for its ornithological excellence but I did seek out the indigenous species and saw many migrants.

Madeira and its sister island Porto Santo are the remains of ancient volcanoes thrown up a few million years ago from the seabed far out in the Atlantic. Madeira is very mountainous with peaks rising to 1,862 metres divided by rugged valleys descending to a rocky coast. After heavy rainfall, which is not infrequent, it is a land of spectacular waterfalls; old streams are quickly swollen into mighty rivers and new streams splash over rock faces like curtains of lace.

There are few birds of prey – the ubiquitous Barn Owl breeds here and the Short-eared Owl is a regular migrant. But the Canaries Kestrel is always around; it hovered seldom but swooped amongst the pine trees and occasionally roosted on one of them, heralding its approach with a shrill cry like a wire being twanged. There is a Madeira Sparrow Hawk and a Madeira Buzzard, both of which are probably sub-species.

Canaries are very common but they are green rather than yellow and I saw many flitting about the gardens of Funchal or perched and singing their sweet notes. There were flocks of sparrows quarrelling and chattering noisily but these were Spanish Sparrows which are identified by the white cheeks of the male and the chestnut crown; the other sparrows we saw were Rock Sparrows, which are paler brown and the white spots on top of the tip of the tail may be discerned. Other finches which breed

here are: Greenfinch, Goldfinch, Chaffinch and Linnet. All these we saw but not the Hawfinch, which is only an accidental.

I was fortunate to see a small flock of Firecrests in the bushes by the roadside on the way to Porto da Cruz. This bird is a rare migrant in Britain which I had not previously seen in England, although it may be found in France, Italy and Portugal. This tiny bird is slightly larger than the Goldcrest with the same gold coloured crown, but distinguished from it by contrasting black and white stripes above the eye which is similar in both sexes. Its upper parts are green with a yellow tinge on each side of the head and shoulders. There are only four species in the genus *Regulus*, of which the Goldcrest and Firecrest are both known in Europe; the other two are the Ruby-crowned Knight and the Golden-crowned Knight, both being North American birds. They are more akin to Warblers than to Wrens.

A local name of the Goldcrest is Kinglet and this is doubtless because of the golden crown and is the origin of the scientific name, *Regulus*, of the genus; the Goldcrest being the archetype; its specific name is *Regulus regulus* and the Firecrest is *Regulus ignicapillus*, referring to its fiery crown. Another name in the vernacular is *basilisk*, which is the Greek word for cockatrice, the fabulous reptile so-called for the mark on its head like a crown. It is also called by seamen 'woodcock's pilot' because the Goldcrest comes to us in Britain from Scandinavia in the autumn, preceding by a few days the Woodcock in their passage across the North Sea. Both species do, however, also breed in our country. Henry Tegner in one of his books describes how he saw a Goldcrest emerge from among the feathers of a Short-eared Owl newly landed from Scandinavia on the Northumbrian coast, having apparently 'thumbed a lift' on the larger bird to cross the North Sea. That must be a formidable journey for such a scrap of life.

Rock Pigeons were flying in and out of caves and landing on ledges of the cliffs all around the coast. These and the Wood Pigeons breed on the island. The words pigeon and dove are generally interchangeable and we know this bird as the Rock Dove which is alleged to be the ancestor of all domestic pigeons. It is essentially a coastal bird in Britain, but widely spread in

Firecrest

Southern Europe, being larger than the Wood Pigeon. A friend showed me out of his fridge a Long-toed Pigeon, which he called a 'Laurel Pigeon', and which he intended to have mounted. This also was larger than a Wood Pigeon and dark grey in colour. Its claws were demonstrably longer than normal but whether the other species is due to its preference for roosting in laurel bushes I was not able to discover. Both are Palearctic birds but I think it was the Long-toed (*Columba trocaz.*)

There were many swifts streaking across the sky in the early mornings and again in the evenings. They always took flight at the same time each evening at about 16.00 hours local time and continued hunting and screaming until 18.00 hours when they disappeared just as suddenly. This is the Pallid Swift which breeds here as also does the Little Black Swift. The Barn Swallows and House Martins are also plentiful in winter but these all fly north to breed. The behaviour of the Pallid Swift is just the same as that of our familiar Swift, *Apus apus*, but it is paler in colour and has more white on the throat.

Both the Blackbird and the Redbreast breed in Madeira and look identical to our species at home. Both cock and hen Blackbirds were common in the parks and gardens, often in pairs, but I saw no evidence of nest-building or feeding young; the cock started singing very beautifully at dawn.

Of all the many warblers I expected to see, I saw only two, the Blackcap which was often singing in the parks and gardens and the Spectacled Warbler, both of which breed here. The former has a pleasant sustained warble and the latter a shorter and more subdued song. The Blackcap is a strong enough flier to make the long sea journey but both breed and winter here. The Willow and Wood Warblers are regular winter visitors, migrating from Europe into this warmer climate but they breed in the north. Other warblers claimed by Madeira are accidentals blown here by strong winds.

Of game birds only the Partridge and the Quail are indigenous, unless we include the Woodcock which also breeds here but I always think is too nice a bird to be shot. Both the Red-legged Partridge which we often call at home the Frenchman, and the

Barn Owl

archetype, of which the male has the black horseshoe on its chest and one which Americans call the Hungarian Partridge, breed here. I suspect, however, that the latter is probably the Barbary Partridge, which is easily confused unless one sees the black horseshoe, which I did not. Old records in Madeira show bags of partridge of as many as seventy falling to a single gun and one man still living says he himself shot thirty-two in a single day; no such bags could be achieved today and it would appear that these two species have been grossly over-shot. Both the Ringed Plover and the Lesser Ringed Plover breed in Madeira, which are very much alike unless seen at close quarters; and the Kentish Plover, which frequents all the coasts of southern Europe, also breeds in this island; the other Plovers seen on the few sandy beaches are all migrants.

Of course, there is an abundance of sea birds and the main island is so narrow that one is never far from the sea and thus from sea birds. The Herring Gull is numerous and bold, even swooping down to steal breakfast set out on hotel balconies. It, and the Lesser Blackback, the Kittiwakes, and the Black-headed Gulls are all noisy and plentiful around the coast, but the latter has lost its brown head, which is prominent in the breeding season. Of Terns, we have the Common breeding and the Roseate is suspected of nesting here also but the evidence is uncertain. Of more interest are the petrels and shearwaters; these are best seen on Porto Santo when they come ashore at night whilst incubating or feeding young. The petrels were seen at sea, skimming in the troughs of the waves but I never saw them ashore; the Fork-tailed and the Bulwer's Petrels breed here so they were probably either or both.

High up on the north facing slope near to Pico da Junca I did see some shearwaters and these could have been the Manx Shearwater or the Little Shearwater, both of which have sharply pointed wings and tubular nostrils on top of the bills. Cory's Shearwater also breeds here but this is larger and not easily confused. The Soft-plumaged Petrel, which has been recorded not only in the Palearctic Region, but also in the Tropical, Ethiopian, and Australasian Regions, does definitely breed on

Porto Santo. My ornithological friend here was adamant that it breeds also on Madeira itself high up on the mountain slopes. Apparently it has a very distinctive call and shepherds there who listened to a tape-recording from Porto Santo swore that they had heard it often on Madeira. Maybe other species may be found to breed here when all local knowledge has been tapped.

Oddly enough no ducks apparently breed here; all the species recorded being migrants. And there are no species of Woodpecker although there are plenty of trees. Herons and Little Egrets are regular visitors and I was happy to see the familiar Grey Wagtail.

On my last day in Funchal I decided to visit the local Natural History Museum to check up on the specific identity of two or three birds I had seen but not identified with certainty and found it more comprehensive than I had been led to suppose. I found rooms devoted to marine life and botany but none on birds so I sought the help of a girl at the reception desk. My limited knowledge of Portuguese was inadequate and she spoke no English but we found a common language in French, which she spoke rather better than I. I asked her to direct me to the ornithological section or bird room. To my surprise she said there was no bird room. I protested because I had been told there was indeed a collection of mounted bird specimens. After a moment's thought she replied, 'Yes, there is a room full of birds but you will not be interested. They are all dead.'

If the conservationists fail in their efforts, I can imagine my great-great-grandchildren asking their parents about birds and being told, 'Yes, there used once to be creatures in this country called birds but they are all dead.'

CHAPTER FIVE

Islands beneath the Wind

Thus the Vikings described the Shetland Islands, a stepping stone on their long voyages to Iceland, Greenland, Newfoundland and the east coast of the United States of America. But Islands of Sheep might have been a better description, for sheep and fish were the livelihood of the hardy Shetlanders until North Sea oil changed everything.

My three friends and I went there to look for something quite different – birds. And we took the easy way there and back for we had just under a week to spare and we could only visit one of the many islands of the archipelago, the one known as Mainland on which the airport is now located. Some of the islands have such splendid names like Fetlar and Unst and Yell that we were sad to miss them.

My friend John not only possessed a house on Mainland but also an aeroplane which he piloted and navigated himself with great skill. This saved much precious time. He brought with him from London another James, a much more famous ornithologist than I; and he collected George and myself from Newcastle airport. We four fitted very comfortably into the aircraft, which was well equipped with all navigation and communication aids and we soon landed at Lerwick. He had a car waiting for us, and after a few formalities to safeguard the aircraft and to ready it for departure four days later, we motored to his house near Levenwick.

This could not have been better located for it stood completely isolated, facing east with a picture window overlooking rough moorland, a small loch and, beyond that, the cliffs and the sea. The room with the picture window was provided with the one essential for such a position, a powerful telescope.

With its aid we quickly located in front of the house several nests of both Arctic and Great Skuas and a Red-throated Diver

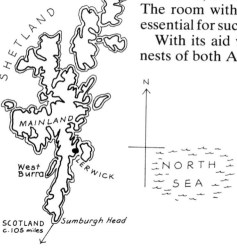

swimming on the loch. We planned a hasty meal and then bird-watching so long as the light lasted. We switched on electricity and opened the fridge to put away the food we had brought with us, only to be met with a horrendous smell. The last occupant of John's house had switched off the power without emptying the fridge; the contents had to be buried hastily.

One of our main objectives in this visit was to see the Great Skua, known locally as the 'bonxie', which is very aggressive. It was nearly extinct in Europe due to egg-collecting, but is now recovering and protected in the Shetlands. Long before we reached the nest he flew straight at us at head height; it was impossible not to duck at the first attack and he cleared our heads by only a few inches. But we learned later to hold our heads resolutely erect when he always tilted his flight upward at the last moment. We filmed this a number of times from different angles; when he is coming directly at the camera it can be very frightening; as he comes in the feet are lowered and claws extended. This is a really big pelagic bird, both sexes are all black except for a white patch on the top of the wings, it is nearly as big as the Great Black-backed Gull, and with an even fiercer hooked bill. The wings are not sharply pointed nor are the central tail feathers extended as in the other three skuas. It is a piratical bird, allowing other sea birds to catch fish and pursuing them with a rapid hawkish flight until they disgorge their catch, which the skua takes in the air. It utters a loud croak in its chase and has been known to swallow small birds whole; it can chase off Ravens and even Golden Eagles. The nest is just a depression trodden in the vegetation and as one approaches it when the female is sitting and the male is away, she will move off the eggs at a good distance and feign injury. She flutters and squawks low to the ground to draw the intruder away from the nest. The two or three eggs are well camouflaged, being olive coloured, so the nest is not easily found amongst grass and heather unless the exact place of her emergence has been observed. She cannot easily be flushed directly from the nest. We put up hides at two nests of the Great Skua and filmed the hen incubating and the cock bird standing on guard about three metres away. He would stand patiently for an

Great Skua

Red-throated Diver

hour or more continuously alert and keeping a look-out all around.

The Arctic Skua is much smaller, being about two-thirds of the size of the Great and is easily recognisable in the air by the extended central tail feather. The two species tolerate each other nesting at no great distance apart. Both sexes are amber coloured in the light phase which is dark brown all over. The Arctic has the same piratical feeding habits and there are many of them in Shetland harrying the gulls and terns and screaming as they give chase; but they are quite capable of catching fish with their hooked black bills and will rob nests of eggs or young.

The Arctic Skua breeds circumpolar and migrates south in winter. In the British Isles it now breeds only in the Hebrides, Orkney and Shetland. It used to breed in Scotland but has been exterminated by gamekeepers. It does not attack humans, as does the Great, but relies upon an elaborate display of feigned injury to draw an intruder away from the nest once eggs have been laid.

We drove down the coast to Sumburgh Head where the lighthouse is poised high on the edge of the great cliff. Puffins were nesting on the grassy slopes on the landward side of the lighthouse wall; from within the wall one could watch them at a few metres' distance and admire their laterally flattened triangular bills with astonishingly bright summer colours of red, blue and yellow. The males sat outside their burrows among the pink flowers of the thrift enjoying the sun and emitting a general murmur of low grunts. They were entirely tame and undisturbed by our proximity.

Flying below us on the other side were Shags, Guillemots, and Razorbills. Far out to sea Gannets were plunging vertically into the ocean.

We motored to a fresh water loch named Tingwall to film the Red-throated Diver and were rewarded with a splendid view of the female swimming up and down this small lochan with a juvenile following close behind her and imitating her every move. They nest on the grassy edge of these inland lochs within a foot or two of the water and there was no cover, so that filming was easy and no hide was needed. This species is much smaller than the Great Northern but similar in shape although the bill is more slender and up-tilted. The upper body is a uniform grey without any pattern and the breast is white. The significant feature is the dark red throat which was very prominent. She did not dive to swim under water to avoid us, as we expected; this was perhaps because the juvenile was not very expert in diving.

We were looking for Whimbrels and located three pairs at West Burna, flying about and making a fuss at our presence. They nest on the ground like Curlews and probably had eggs in the nests so we did not attempt to find them. Their call is a lovely bubbling sound, more rapid and more musical than that of the Curlew, whose spring call I have always thought to be one of the loveliest sounds in nature.

The Black Guillemot is a winter visitor to the Farne Islands, which we know well, and not very common at that, so we were anxious to see this species and to study its breeding habits. We found a pair nesting in a steep cleft in the cliffs near to Sandwich, which we could readily watch but not reach. The female was sitting on its single egg but the male often came out onto a ledge, which gave us a splendid view. He is much like our familiar Guillemot but somewhat smaller and all black in colour except for white patches on top of the wings and vivid red feet and gape. These latter are most striking when seen from above as he is swimming or in passing fish to his mate. His sound is very different from the grunt of the Guillemot, being a whistling or trilling cry.

We were fortunate to see a pair of Red-breasted Mergansers on the Loch of Tingwall, which must have had their nest on one of the small islands in the loch, but we did not locate it. The drake in breeding plumage is a particularly handsome bird with his black head and back, white collar and chestnut head and neck and a white throat; both have the distinctive double crest projecting from the back of the head. She is very like the female Goosander in colouring but the crest of the latter is single. They are both 'sawbills' with the narrow serrated bill which enables them to hold onto fish once caught under water. In winter they gather into

Black Guillemots

large flocks on estuaries and the sea coast, where they are
excellent swimmers and divers; they tend to move south in a
severe winter.

John, who had been in Shetland in previous summers, knew of
a ternery on a sandy slope of the shore; but when we visited it
there was not a tern to be seen, nor any sign of nesting. By
watching the flight of terns inland from various directions
carrying sand eels and small fish in their bills; we concluded that
they had been disturbed from their traditional breeding site and
we determined to find the new area. Eventually we located it near
to the centre of Mainland, high up on the hill, and between two
radar stations. The ground was covered with the scrapes of Arctic
and Common Terns, each containing two eggs. We estimated
there to be five to six hundred nests. The air was filled with their
discordant cries and we felt that our discovery of their new
breeding ground was much resented so we did not linger there. A
pair of Ravens tumbled about the air and we knew that any eggs
left unguarded would be stolen by them. We pitied the poor
precocial chicks when they would wander from parental care.

There was a pair of Wheatears nesting in the dry stone wall
which formed a sheep pen in front of the house and they were
feeding young, which provided me with an excellent opportunity
to film them flying to and fro with food. The name, which has
nothing to do with the cereal or the birds' ears, is said to be
derived from the direct Anglo-Saxon name, *white earse*, meaning
'white rump' and this is the feature which instantly attracts
attention; the rump and sides of the tail in both sexes are vivid
white, contrasting with the buff breast and belly. The male has a
grey back, with a black tip to the tail, a black eye stripe and black
wing coverts. They were both assiduous in feeding the young
every few minutes, with frequent clicking notes to keep in touch.

All four of us were watching the Red-necked Phalarope darting
amongst reeds when an elderly farmer stopped his tractor to
comment that this species used to be more plentiful in his youth.
In conversation with him John learned that he had, in his younger
days, been in the merchant fleet like many Shetlanders, in order
to save enough to buy a small farm. It emerged that he had sailed

Wheatear

with the shipowners of which John is Chairman, and he was delighted to hear of this connection. To add to his surprise John then pointed to one of us and told him that this man was the Chairman of Furness Withy, then one of the largest shipowners in the world. The individual concerned was intent on watching the Phalarope and clad in an open-necked shirt and shorts. At this astonishing news the farmer nearly fell off his tractor. 'Can that man be the Chairman of Furness Withy?' he gasped. Clearly he had imagined such a position to demand a tail coat, striped trousers and a top hat. It must have been a source of great disillusion to him.

Next day we did return to the City and, if not to tail coat and top hat, at least to more sombre clothing. We left the house on the shore tidier than we found it, with nothing in the fridge; and we swept up the muddy footmarks we had imprinted on the carpets. John, who had certainly never handled a carpet-sweeper before in his life, was entranced by its efficiency and kept muttering about the delights of housekeeping as a foil to bird watching, but I feared it would pall. He piloted us safely back to Aberdeen where some of us went by helicopter onto an oil rig. About mid-ocean I observed that two of my companions were fast asleep and John, flying on instruments and a beam was extremely drowsy; I wondered if I could land the plane if none of them woke up in time, or whether my extensive field notes and films would be lost to posterity.

CHAPTER SIX

La Camargue

In our first morning in Les Baux I woke to the fluting call of the Golden Oriole. Looking from the narrow bedroom window, I saw him perched on top of the cypress hedge in the hotel garden. Later we found the nest high up in the hedge, slung below a forked branch. It was my first sight of this bird and his brilliant yellow and black plumage was as vivid as that of any tropical bird.

We had gathered at our rendezvous late in the previous evening, Eric and I by air from London to Marseille, David by air from Basle, and my daughter by car from Geneva. But she was only to stay for two days. The time and place had been arranged many weeks previously.

Eric's and my journey from the airport was not without incident: a friend had arranged a hired car to be available for us at the airport which proved to be a Peugeot; he kindly awaited our arrival and handed me the keys. He offered to lead us onto a main road but was obviously in a hurry to depart to keep another appointment. No sooner had we put our luggage into the boot than he had started and we had to leap into the Peugeot, find the ignition and starter, and hasten to keep his car in sight. It was, of course, a left-hand drive, to which I was not accustomed, and I had to discover the controls and gears by trial and error – mostly error! Soon he stopped at a major road where he indicated our route by a wave of the arm. We jumped out and thanked him and then he departed hastily, leaving us to work out the rest of our journey from the map. On the motorway we were behind a huge articulated truck which changed down several gears to negotiate a long hill. I could see nothing ahead so pulled out gently to the left to look around the obstruction and hastily pulled in again because a car was hurtling down the hill like a bullet. This car must have been travelling at well over 100 m.p.h., it swerved quite unnecessarily and almost overturned. It rocked from side to side

with screaming brakes and almost went over the precipice at the far side of the road but stopped at the brink. I also stopped and crossed the road on foot and in peril of my life to be sure it was able to proceed. The driver was unhurt but angry. I explained we were English and not familiar with driving on the right. He said we were fools and should not be allowed on the road. With these mutual expressions of goodwill, we parted before we initiated a pile-up of all the downhill traffic which appeared to be intent on suicide.

It was a bad start to our bird-watching expedition and I felt a bit shaken but Eric was quite unperturbed. Our destination was Les Baux, an ancient village lying between Arles and Tarascon. I had intended to book rooms in the Julius Caesar Hotel in Arles, which is closer to the Camargue in the delta of the Rhone, but my friend in Marseille insisted that we should stay in L'Osteau de Baux Maniere; though situated north of Arles and thus a little more distant from our objective, it would prove to be well worth the extra travel. He did not say that its merit lay in its fantastic gastronomic reputation which had earned it all the crossed knives and forks in the Michelin Guide and to indulge in which delights of superb food and wine justified French families journeying many hundreds of kilometres for a single meal.

We skirted Arles and took a minor road, D.17, which led us into a valley leading up into the hills. The scenery became increasingly fantastic in the failing light as we climbed towards the head of the valley which was seemingly a dead end. On our right rose a steep cliff with the ancient Moorish village of Les Baux on top of it and directly ahead another cliff with the hotel crouched at its foot. On all sides were great blocks of white limestone as big as houses or tower blocks, which proved to be remnants of cliffs quarried by man over centuries.

In our anxiety to avoid sudden death on the race track of the highway and to follow our map on the lesser roads we had little opportunity to look out for birds, but we narrowly avoided hitting a cock Pheasant which is our familiar game bird; it is ominously named locally *faisan de chasse*, and hunted it certainly is. There were Swallows still hawking insects in the fading light and Eric's keen eyes identified this as our Barn Swallow from Africa and not the Red-rumped Swallow we had expected it to be. We heard Turtle Doves and a Cuckoo but that was the limit of our ornithological studies on that day. The ensuing days were to prove very different!

We received a fine welcome at the hotel and there were David and Katharine just recently arrived from two different origins.

In order to make a sensible plan so that we might use our available time to the best advantage we visited the headquarters of the National Nature Reserve – Centre d'Ecologie de Camargue, to which Eric had an introduction, and we presented our credentials. We were well received and, when we had defined our purpose, were introduced to an impressive heavily bearded man in an office already well filled with mounted specimens of birds which barely left room for us. He had an encyclopaedic knowledge of the local birds, which he shared with us most generously. He made space on his crowded desk to allow us to spread out our large-scale maps and thereon we noted where best to look for the species we particularly hoped to see. This knowledge saved us many hours of searching and of re-tracing our steps many times over.

We had planned to call upon the most eminent figure in natural history in the Camargue and of international fame – Dr Lukas Hoffman, the founder of the Biological Research Institute of La Tour du Valat, who had purchased a vast area of the Camargue wetlands and put it into a Trust to save its wildlife and habitat from commercial exploitation. Our host advised us to make this the starting point of our exploration and offered to telephone Dr Hoffman to enquire if it would be convenient for us to call upon him at once. It was.

We found our way to La Tour du Valat which is both his home and the headquarters of the Trust. He received us kindly in his office and talked about the effect of tourists on the wetlands and the work of the World Wildlife Fund, of which he is one of the founders and has been President. He is a great naturalist and a great man, who has put a vast amount of his knowledge and time and personal wealth into the study and preservation of wildlife.

He introduced us to some of the students working on projects in the field and the laboratory, several of whom were British. And then he very kindly led us by car to a swampy field on his estate to view a breeding colony of Black-winged Stilts and other rarities. The Stilts presented a memorable sight; there were more than sixty nests projecting from the shallow water or built on grassy hummocks and those we examined had eggs. The parent birds left the nests at our approach and wheeled about in the sky with a clamour of shrill cries, their extraordinarily long pink legs stretching far behind their tails.

They made a glorious pattern as they flew, with their solid black wings and brilliant white bodies; the few males could be distinguished by having some black at the back of the head. When some birds landed at a distance from us, they waded in the shallow water with long strides.

On another site Dr Hoffman showed us a colony of Whiskered Terns numbering about sixty pairs; and there were a few White-winged Terns breeding amongst them. He drew our attention to the chick of a Slender-billed Gull, so there must have been a few of these Gulls nesting in the ternery, although we did not see the adults. These two species of terns were new to us and the White-winged Black Tern is a rarity in Europe.

On a pool passed on our journey we observed three Gadwall drakes in breeding plumage which usually breed in Europe east of France. It was a very good day for us.

Next day we decided to look at the old town of Les Baux on the summit of the high cliff and so ascended the steep and winding road which led to it. This was a Moorish stronghold and history tells us that they killed their captives by throwing them over the precipice. We spent the rest of the day in the adjacent hill country, Les Alpilles, to watch some of the inland birds.

Alpine Swifts and Crag Martins were two new species for me. The former are larger and brown in colour rather than black, as are the Swifts of home; they have a white belly and a longer forked tail; but their flight and habits are similar. The Crag Martin is not found at all in northern Europe; it is not too different from our Sand Martin but has a wedge-shaped tail.

Black-winged Stilt

Overhead we saw two Bonelli's Eagles, identified by the white breast and dark underwings of the adult at no great height. There is a very obvious dark band across the end of the tail when viewed from below. Its companion appeared to be a juvenile, which had no white breast but was brown on tail and underparts. We watched them awhile hoping to see one or other stoop onto a rabbit but neither did. There was also a Honey Buzzard in the sky above us, a smaller bird with a shorter wing span; this also has dark bars under the tail and a longer neck than our Buzzard, which we see in Cumbria. Eric suggested it must be a late migrant on its way to breed further north.

Here were numerous warblers flitting and singing amongst the gorse and other scrub bushes, difficult to identify by sight except at close quarters and more easily recognised by their songs. Eric is an expert in this identification and pointed out to us the Dartford Warbler, the Orphean Warbler and the Subalpine Warbler and, very specially, the Marmora's Warbler. We had a close view of this latter bird, hitherto unknown in this area, preening on a dead twig in full sunlight. It was a uniform slate-grey, paler on belly and darker on the crown, wings and throat. The red eye-ring is obvious. Eric reported this later to *Ibis* as a probable first sight in the Camargue.

We saw a Black Redstart, which is seen in England only in the southern counties, and which has the same unmistakable flirt of the rusty red tail as the Redstart we know at home. It was the cock but not nearly so colourful as our local bird, being uniformly black except for the white wing-patch and rusty tail and rump. It perched on a rock and its tail flickered constantly up and down.

On our return to the hotel we added to our first sightings the smallest of finches, the Serin, and we located its tiny nest in the cypress hedge in the garden. This is a streaked yellow bird, like a Siskin, but smaller and with no black on the crown of the male. He sang from the very top of one of the bushes while his mate incubated the eggs in a nest too high up in the hedge for us to examine.

The Camargue is the only place in Europe where Flamingos breed and then not every year. They like brackish water of a suitable depth and the degree of salinity has to be just right for them. This year it had been reported that flocks of the Greater Flamingo were nesting on their usual lagoon and we had looked forward to filming them. However, Dr Hoffman asked us not to go there because the strong wind, the Mistral, was blowing hard, which would blow any young birds disturbed from their nest far from the breeding site to be lost by their parents and to die of starvation. They had been so disturbed this year and the result was disastrous. Of course, we respected his wish; he told us the adults were feeding in the Etang de Vaccares and we could film them there if we could approach sufficiently near.

These large and beautiful birds raise a heap of mud from the bottom of a shallow lake so that the top of the hummock projects a few inches above the surface of the water. On this the hen lays her single egg. The young were already hatched so we could not have seen how she disposes her exceptionally long legs.

On the third day of our stay we went to the Etang de Vaccares and were delighted to see a flock of Great Flamingo feeding in the water near the farther shore. At no small cost of wading and pushing through dense undergrowth and tormented by squadrons of mosquitoes, we made a detour and emerged on the shore in their proximity. They had already moved out towards the middle and although we had just peered through the salicornia bushes from a prone position, they had become sufficiently aware of our presence to keep moving steadily away from us, feeding all the while with wide sweeps of their massive beaks through the bottom mud like a team of harvesters scything the standing corn.

It was agreed that I should make another detour to reach a finger of land covered with tamarisk trees that pointed towards the flock whilst my two friends would stand on the shore to engage their attention. By this device I was able to approach within 100 metres and obtained some fine pictures. Then I tried to shorten the distance and this was too much for them. With a great clamour of their enormous wings threshing the water and loud honking cries the whole flock rose into the air and flew off to some other source of food.

In the water they were a lovely vision of pink and white bodies, long red legs up to the ankles in the green water, and long white necks arched down to the water with head and huge curved bill submerged. Seen from below they were even more impressive; the great wings revealed bright crimson and black underneath; the head and neck stretched forward; and the amazing red legs trailed out as far behind. We all stood awe-stricken by this wonderful sight.

The other birds we noted on the water at Vaccares were not strangers to us but well worth recording – a single Pintail drake, several Coots, and a few Common Pochard and Red-crested Pochard. Mallard were plentiful on every stretch of water; and every reed bed had a Marsh Harrier patrolling methodically up and down like a hound following a scent.

On the following morning we spent two hours in Arles looking at the splendid Roman forum and other relics and then took the road to Aigues Mortes. This journey was taken not only to see that unique mediaeval walled town but also to view the heronry in the tall trees on the way to it, where we might expect to see not only the Grey Heron at the nest, but also the Little Egret and the Night Heron. This is probably the northern limit of the Little Egret's breeding as it is an African bird; they had built their nests of sticks lower on the trees than the Herons and they made a fine sight of glistening white with a slender drooping crest of white feathers, greatly favoured at one time by milliners, which fashion threatened their existence. In flight their yellow feet at the end of black legs are very obvious. There were a few Cattle Egrets evidently breeding in the same colony, but these could be seen everywhere feeding on the ground at the feet of the black cattle; other than by their feeding habits they are not easy to distinguish but their legs and feet are all black. A Squacco Heron was also seen with pink legs and pale buff plumage; one or two pairs of this species may well have been nesting in the same heronry. We saw the stumpy form of the black and white Night Heron on several occasions crouched in ditches but we never saw it in flight. We had a good view of a Bittern near Cachel, which was flying laboriously by day, having been disturbed from among the reeds at the roadside. We saw another hidden amongst reeds at the

Night Heron

Marais de Romley and also a Night Heron quite near to it.

We pressed on to see Aigues Mortes, which proved to be well worthy of a visit. Children were playing *boules* on the green outside the massive entrance where we left our car, having been warned that the streets within the walls are too narrow to accommodate it. By ascending steps to the top of these walls one can see the whole town of crowded houses and narrow streets. This is alleged to have been a 'jumping-off point' for Crusaders taking ship to the Holy Land and we were told there used to be a canal by which ships came close to the town. At one corner of the wall was an iron cage in which, I suppose, malefactors used to be exposed to their death for some crime or heresy. Not a pleasant way to die in the summer heat.

On the return journey we saw a Roller sitting on a telephone wire. We stopped to watch it for some minutes until it flew off, when we hoped we might see the roll in flight, which is part of the male bird's nuptial display but it was probably too late in the breeding season for this spectacle. We do not see this lovely bird in Britain except as a very occasional vagrant, it is larger than a Mistle Thrush with vivid blue plumage and chestnut back. At first glance we had mistaken it for the Blue Rock Thrush, which was also on our list of birds we hoped to see and so we spent the rest of the afternoon searching for that species among the foothills around Les Baux, which is the ideal habitat. In this we were unsuccessful and indeed never saw one, which was odd because they are not uncommon. On the following evening the menu for our dinner contained a new dish – paté of thrushes – we knew where our Rock Thrushes had gone! But we had seen Crested Larks and Skylarks, so our time was not wasted.

We dined sumptuously each evening in the Osteau de Beaumaniere. The menu was usually the same each evening, each dish being a speciality of the house and famous throughout France – lobster soup, blue trout, and guinea fowl with superb wines with each. There were alternatives but this was our usual choice out of a menu sheet measuring about a metre square. After a few evenings of careful study it needed only a glance at it to make our choice and as we were living demi-pension, the cost

Rock Thrushes

of each separate dish, though formidably high, was irrelevant for us. It was a similar situation when choosing wines; the wine waiter, complete with leather apron and a small wooden ladle on his lapel, followed the head waiter with his menu after a decent interval of half an hour to discuss the wines after the dishes had been chosen. We had benefited from intimate discussion with him on the first three evenings and had followed his advice with excellent results so that we needed only to quote a number to him when he came for our order.

The dining-room, which in my recollection resembles a cave, was always completely filled but we never saw the same guests twice. Most of the family parties of two and three generations came for the evening meal and had travelled great distances for it. The menu was consulted whilst drinking aperitifs in the adjoining bar and was the subject of excited chatter by young and old. When the vital decisions had been made and orders given, attention was turned to the wine list and intense discussion held with the wine-waiter. This was less excited and indeed reverent but finally the drinks were also agreed and a hush of anticipation fell upon each group. It was then that I often intercepted a pitying glance or overheard a whispered comment about the ignorant and barbarous Englishmen who paid such scant attention to choosing either the food or wine. We never saw much of these fellow diners who were engrossed in their enjoyment of their dinner which continued into the late evening when probably we had retired wearily to bed. We rose early and were always alone at our simple breakfast of coffee and rolls. The sleepy waiter who served us looked upon us with pity as we hastened to be on our way. On the first Sunday morning he appeared to be still clearing up the gastronomic revels of the night before and looked utterly astonished to see us equipped for the road. 'Do you have to work even on Sundays?' he asked us in his local patois and extreme pity.

Luncheon was always a simple meal for us taken briefly at whatever hour suited our bird studies. We took it in turn to buy food in any village we passed through. It always consisted of a long loaf of bread, a bottle of rough red wine (with a loose cork and no label) a piece of cheese and fruit of some kind. On one very memorable day we ate this seated on the sand dunes beside a salt water marsh, the Radeau de la Tamisse. Eric, who is a very famous artist, was making rapid pencil sketches of Kentish Plovers feeding in the shallow water near our feet. He made many sketches of single birds and groups in a variety of postures with scribbled references to colours, light and reflection.

I learned later how he would work these up into the wonderful water-colour pictures for which he is so renowned. He has very keen eyesight and an amazing memory for detail so that his pictures are quite unique and much sought after. His bird pictures are alive and the subjects might run to take cover at any second. Moreover, he has such a profound knowledge of bird anatomy that the skeleton, the muscles, and the sinews are all apparent to him and give that vitality to his pictures which differ so widely from those painted from mounted specimens.

I learned later from his work in the studio with what infinite care but simple materials and equipment his genius produces these splendid records of what his trained eyes have seen and his skilled hand has sketched. As much attention is given also to background, reflection, and light source. He chooses a tinted paper with an appropriate texture (often chosen from his collection of old envelopes) to avoid colour-washing a whole sheet of white cartridge paper. Onto the rim of a simple enamel plate he squeezes a spot of each of the few colours he will need. He washes each down into the bottom of the plate with plenty of water, mixing into the shades of his choice. Then the colours are floated onto the paper in a clean wash. Highlights and particular flashes of colour are added as, for instance, a red bill or a dark eye-stripe. To watch him at work is an education in confident skill of eye and hand combined with a profound knowledge of his subject.

He sketched not only the Kentish Plover on that day but also that elegant bird, the Avocet, which always adopts postures and forms groups which seem ideal for the artist and photographer. For many years this beautiful black and white water bird with its long blue legs and slender decurved bill had ceased to breed in

Avocet

Britain but was quite recently attracted back to breed in a sanctuary in East Anglia where it is now well established as a breeding species. It does breed in Holland and southern Spain in estuaries and mudflats and is common in many parts of Africa. It feeds by sweeping its bill from side to side as it wades through shallow water. This bird is always a joy to watch and must be a joy to sketch.

Some little Wagtails were running about on the sand at the water's edge which we at first took to be our familiar Yellow Wagtail that breeds in U.K. but migrates to the Mediterranean and all down the west coast of Africa. On closer examination by binocular, however, we saw that it was the Blue-headed Wagtail, which is the European race of the Yellow Wagtail, of which the male has the distinctive blue head and white eye-stripe. All the various races of the Yellow Wagtail do hybridise. In a salicornia bush nearby a Spectacled Warbler had its nest and we were able to identify this warbler by sight with the aid of a binocular because of the white eye-rim, white throat, pink breast, and dark grey head. It could easily have been mistaken for a Whitethroat or Subalpine Warbler.

We moved on to the Radeau de Bamston, another salt water lagoon but with more exposed sand banks or small islands. Here we found several species of Tern nesting so we waded out to see the nests and eggs more closely. I have a clear mental picture of Eric's stocky figure wading knee-deep between the islands with a stout stick in one hand and a binocular in the other. The Terns wheeled above us in a clamorous cloud, diving at Eric's thinly covered head but never actually drawing blood. He ignored their attacks completely, being intent on identifying the different species in the air and then the eggs in their scrapes in the sand. The Gull-billed Terns and Sandwich Terns were nesting in the same colony and could only be distinguished by the former having no yellow tip to the black bill and no crest at the back of the black head. The Common Terns, only slightly smaller, also have a black head but the bill is bright red with a black tip. The other species there was the Little Tern, markedly smaller in size than the others and having a yellow bill with a black tip. These sharp differences in bill colouring during the breeding season must surely enable the sexes to recognise their own species and thus to avoid inter-breeding. Their egg colourings do differ slightly and somehow they seem able to find their own nests after leaving them when disturbed. But almost immediately after hatching the precocial young run around anywhere in the colony and how the parents can be sure they are feeding their own offspring is a mystery. Certainly the young do ardently pursue any adult carrying sand eels.

When we reluctantly returned to the shore we found an angry farmer menacing us with a shotgun, and shouting incoherently. He pointed to a notice which read *'Chasse Privée'* and we told him in our best French that we were not shooting but only taking photographs. The idea of anyone troubling to wade out to the islands merely to take photographs seemed incomprehensible to him but eventually we escaped unscathed.

The fact that our bird-watching visit and the celebrated procession and ceremony at Sainte Marie de la Mer coincided was fortuitous. But, being there, we decided to forego birding that day and to see this rare spectacle of the gypsy festival which is so famous. We reached the village at an early hour, parked the car, and entered the old church to fill in the time. We were not alone. Gypsy women in brightly coloured dresses came and went. In the crypt one young woman was lost in passionate prayer to the image of the Christ Child mounted on the wall, tears streaming down her face. From her movements and her gabbled words we guessed she was pleading to be blessed with a child or perhaps with a male child. We hastened to leave her, hoping that her prayers would be answered.

Along the sea-front gypsies were gathering, having come, we learned, in their hundreds from all the shores of the Mediterranean. This is an ancient festival to celebrate the legend that Mary, the Mother of Jesus, brought the Holy Child in a boat from Palestine to a landfall at this village. Each year a procession takes the image of the black Christ to immerse in the sea at the legendary place of landing.

The main street and the foreshore were already filling up with

Lesser Grey
Shrike

local people and tourists. Dark-skinned gypsies were every-where; tall, handsome black-haired men and women in bright clothes, and there were scores of children. Some women were telling the fortunes of visitors by reading their palms; some children were begging with outstretched hands – probably from habit as these people showed no signs of poverty. There were donkeys and a few ponies in evidence but the gypsies had travelled in saloon cars pulling trailers or in luxurious motor-caravans. There were Cadillacs among the cars. But the old vagabond way of life had not been entirely discarded; tents had been pitched alongside the road on the sand dunes; hens pecked among the grass but each was tethered by one leg to the car bumper.

The crowd was beginning to concentrate on the side-walks of the main street so we joined it. Presently the head of the procession reached us. It included men on white horses with their black 'cowboy' hats and a group of splendid women in the traditional dresses of Arles. In the midst was a float ornamented with flowers and bearing the image of the Virgin Mary and the Christ Child. The spectators joined the tail of the procession and we went with them. After walking a few hundred metres along the road they crossed the sand and waded into the sea waist deep. The horsemen and the ladies of Arles were much in evidence surrounding the immersion ceremony so that we could not well see what happened.

We saw a Spotted Flycatcher on our way back to the car; it was a late migrant heading north.

We sat one day on the hillside overlooking a vineyard and there was a bird perched upon almost every post. Each darted off at intervals to seize a passing insect and returned to its perch; we had ample opportunity to identify them as four different species of Shrike. There was also a Kestrel hovering overhead but it was not the rarer Lesser Kestrel that we hoped to see. The Shrikes are the so-called 'butcher birds' which impale their captured prey upon thorns to be devoured later; these constitute their larder. The biggest of these was the Great Grey Shrike, a handsome black, grey and white bird with a strong hooked bill and a long tail in perpetual motion. In that location it seemed to concentrate on the larger insects but it also takes small ground mammals and lizards. It can occasionally be seen in U.K. but not breeding.

The Lesser Grey Shrike is not found in U.K. but there were several in the vineyard and seeing the two species together made identification easy by comparison of size; the colouring and markings are very similar to the Great Grey, but the tail is relatively shorter; it occasionally hovers like the Kestrel. There were two male Red-backed Shrikes, of which the back and wings are coloured chestnut, heads and rumps grey, with a black eye-stripe, and pinkish breast. And the Woodchat Shrike was also present with its deep-chestnut head and nape in the cock and overall brown plumage in the hen. We watched them for an hour because it was so unusual to see the four species together.

The name Shrike was first seen in English in mid sixteenth century but seems to have referred to the Mistlethrush. The Shrikes were called Butcher Birds. The word Shrike comes from the Old Norse word *skrikja* and this is preserved in modern Swedish as *skrika*. But this name is applied in Sweden to the Jay. It is all very confusing. The German name for Shrike is more akin to our Butcherbird.

Near at hand was the Marais de Saliers where we had been told we might see Pratincole. We were prepared for a long vigil but hardly had we parked the car and seated ourselves unobtrusively behind a wall than we had a splendid view of several hawking for insects like swallows quite close above our heads. This was my first sight of this lovely bird which visits England only very occasionally and never breeds with us. In shape and flight it is just like a Swallow with deeply forked tail but, of course, much larger. The plumage is, however, very different; on top it is a greenish brown and below it is white but the throat is a pinkish cream and the throat patch is bordered with a very distinct black line. They uttered a twittering note as they flew. It was a gorgeous sight to lie back to watch the new (to us) species so close, so oblivious to our presence.

Another day was devoted to a search for the Stone Curlew, which is a wader, but not belonging to the same genus as the

Curlew. It is sometimes named the 'thick-knee', which is perhaps a better name. We had been advised to look for this bird on a stony desert area shown on our map as La Crau. This seemed a hopeless task for the area is vast and featureless and the bird we sought is furtive, skulking among the scant vegetation. Its colouring is sandy, which provides good camouflage. Only in flight is it easily seen. However, we stopped our car every few hundred metres to scan the ground with three powerful binoculars. We did see on the roadside a male Great Spotted Cuckoo and this was rewarding because there are twelve different species of Cuckoo world-wide but only one of these, our familiar Cuckoo, is a summer visitor to Britain.

The other is a summer visitor to southern Europe only; both are polyandrous and brood-parasitic. This practice of laying eggs in other birds' nests and thus opting out of the obligations of parenthood is the feature most people remember about the Cuckoo but there are several other species which adopt the same despicable habit. The other memorable feature is the distinctive and onomatopoeic name for that oft-repeated cry in the early mornings of summer which is not always welcome after the first week. This is the call of the male and many people fail to recognise the answer of the female, which is a prolonged bubbling note. The female is very like the male in appearance, slate grey with a barred breast, but occasionally one may see a rufus-coloured female, reddish brown on top, cream below, and strongly barred all over, which might be mistaken for a Kestrel.

But the Great Spotted Cuckoo, at which we were now looking and which obligingly remained seated at the roadside until we moved nearer, is a bigger bird, brown above and flecked with white, a very obvious white crest, white throat, and a black tail edged with white, which never cries 'cuckoo' under any circumstances.

We had a distant view of a Montagu's Harrier in flight, which is not commonly seen in the Camargue and we relied upon Eric's identification as it is not readily distinguishable from the Hen Harrier. Two other birds new to David and myself were seen in the air – the Short-toed Lark, of which we saw several, and

Montagu's Harrier

Stone Curlew

Calandra Lark which we saw circling and singing high above us.

But then we saw the bird we had come to see in that habitat – the Stone Curlew. I am not usually the first to see a bird or to locate a nest, in fact it is unusual for me to do either. We were all scanning the stony ground between us and the horizon in three different areas. Suddenly, at the limit of my vision in the circle of my binocular lenses as a tiny image clear in the glare of sunlight, a Stone Curlew in a crouched position was creeping furtively back to its nest. It was an exciting moment for me and my first view of this interesting bird.

Eric said 'Don't take your eyes off it!' and I latched them on and did not dare even to blink. He said he would walk to the place some 400 metres distant and which he could not see, for the bird had flattened herself on the eggs and had become invisible at this range. I was to direct him by hand signals, which I did. Soon he raised an arm to indicate he could see the sitting bird, which then stealthily moved off the eggs and merged into the scanty vegetation. David and I hastened to join him. The nest was a mere scrape in the ground in which lay two oval eggs, a dull cream colour spotted and streaked with grey and brown, perfectly camouflaged. The bird I saw so clearly as it left the eggs, crouching furtively with its head flattened to the ground, was probably the male which does most of the incubating. We did not stay for more than two minutes to take a few still photographs so as to allow the bird to return to the eggs, which were probably near to hatching. We watched from the car in hope of a better view of the bird, but he would not return to the eggs whilst we were in view.

The Stone Curlew used to be quite common in southern England, being migrant from the Mediterranean area, but is now seen only in the south-east near the coast. It is a large and bulky bird with long yellow legs, a short yellow bill with a black tip, a white stripe below the eye and a black stripe through it. The overall plumage is in colour sandy with streaks of brown which renders it almost invisible in such a habitat. I looked for the 'thick-knee', for which it is sometimes named but this feature was not obvious to my brief view of it approaching the nest. I learned later that it is the young bird of this species which have swollen leg joints to account for the name 'thick-knee'.

We continued to look out for the Lesser Kestrel which is not found in U.K. It is a smaller bird than the Kestrel but this difference in size is not noticeable unless the two species are seen in proximity. However, the distinguishing feature is the rufous plumage on the back of the male bird, which is not spotted as it is in the Kestrel. We had been directed to Mount Majour as a certain nesting site but sadly could not see them there. A local farmer told us that they had been ejected by Jackdaws from their traditional nest sites in holes in the walls of old buildings and we would find them nesting in cavities on a cliff opposite an old castle at Boulbou. This indeed we did and we saw four pairs busily feeding young on insects caught in flight. Later we saw another pair breeding under the eaves of an old farmhouse near to Le Pebre.

These old farmhouses all had roofs thatched with reeds and upon the ridge of each was a wooden cross inclined at forty-five degrees for the people here are staunch Roman Catholics. When I asked why the cross was always inclined towards the south, I was told it was because of the bitter winds of Protestantism blowing from the north.

A bird we much wanted to see was the Little Bustard and we tramped many miles over likely terrain for a view of them or to find a nest which is always skilfully hidden.

At last when Eric had gallantly left us to make one more trudge over a likely area and David and I had given up and were seated amongst tamarisk bushes, a pair of Little Bustards flew past us at great speed and in full view. This was near a village named Gakons, and we were sad that Eric only saw them at a distance. It is, of course, less than half the size of the Great Bustard but is nevertheless an impressive bird of striking appearance, the male having a bold pattern of black and white on the neck. It is not found at all in U.K. or northern Europe.

We visited the Salin de Badou. There was a large and noisy flock of Arctic Terns breeding on a sand bank of which we counted up to thirty pairs with young on the ground. They looked very splendid in their breeding dress of black crown and vivid red bill, but they are familiar to us breeding on the Farne Islands. In the shallows and on the shore were several Kentish Plovers, which Eric sketched very quickly and cleverly in a variety of attitudes. His particular genius is to see and remember and record the typical stances of flights of every species so that anyone familiar with the bird knows the species in his pictures without looking for the diagnostic markings. Indeed, these are not always visible but Eric paints what he sees and not what he knows from specimens held in the hand as some artists do.

This little wader is only seen on English shores as an occasional vagrant and has to be observed closely to distinguish it from the Ringed Plover and the Little Ringed Plover, both of which do breed with us at home on suitable inland sites of sand or shingle. The legs of the Kentish are black instead of yellow and the black ring on the upper breast is broken at the front.

We had brief glimpses of two other rare birds at this marsh: the Penduline Tit and the Water Rail. It was the peculiar grunting voice of the latter which attracted our attention, without which we would never have noticed it skulking amongst the reeds. As it was, we had very limited sight of it for it is a shy bird and rarely appears in the open. The tiny Penduline Tit has distinctive chestnut colouring and black mark across the eyes; it is not found at all in northern Europe. Again we had only a brief sighting; we searched for its nest which would be suspended from the outer branches of a low bush but failed to find it.

Another bird of which we had only a brief glimpse was the handsome male of the Bearded Reedling, sometimes named the Bearded Tit for, although it is not a true tit, its habits and shape are very like one. It is a colourful bird, the size of a Great Tit but with a much longer tail reminiscent of the Long-tailed Tit. We saw it at the roadside edge of a reed bed and admired its blue head, white breast, and heavy black 'moustaches'. It is certainly not bearded.

We were anxious to find a colony of Bee-eaters for we had seen a number of the highly coloured birds flying singly and purposefully so that we knew there must be a colonial nesting site

Bearded Tit

not far distant. By dint of enquiry amongst local people we did eventually locate it and it was well worth the search. There are several species of Bee-eater in the world, all brightly coloured, but species which breeds in southern Europe and very occasionally in Britain, is the most beautiful of all. It is a motley of blue, green, yellow and chestnut, which is quite dazzling and more resembling a bird of the tropical rain forests. The central tail feathers project like those of an Arctic Skua and the long bill is curved downwards.

Like the Victorian pictures of Waterloo Station, all was bustle and confusion; male and female Bee-eaters look alike and all were feeding young in nests hidden at the end of long tunnels in a vertical bank of red earth. Most of them flew directly and gracefully in and out of the holes but occasionally one would alight on the branches of a nearby tree and this would provide us with a good view of the gorgeous colouring. Probably such hesitation was due to knowledge that the other parent was in the burrow. On the inward trip all birds were carrying insect prey in the bill and many of these were indeed honey bees. There was an apiary not far distant; the colony cannot have been very popular with the bee-keepers.

Nightingales were very plentiful but we heard them rather than saw them. So also were other warblers and we relied upon Eric's intimate knowledge of their songs to differentiate between Blackcap and Garden Warblers in one habitat and the Reed Warbler and Sedge Warbler in another and the Fan-tailed Warbler and Icterine Warbler at La Capelieu. But a Melodious Warbler was clearly identified at Villeneuve on June 1st by its distinctive voice which separates it from the Icterine which it resembles so closely in appearance.

Three weeks was all too short a time to make a real study of this fascinating genus. The time had come for us to leave. The hotel bill gave us all quite a shock and we had to pool all our resources of francs, dollars, sterling and traveller's cheques to meet it. I preserved my watch only by resolution. We left by different flights from Marseille airport for different destinations; David was returning to Basle, for which the airport is just inside the

French border, and he flew Air France. The origin of his flight was in Algeria and it was the time of Algerian independence. At Marseille the plane was already filled with Algerian French being repatriated and much emotion. He secured a seat beside an Algerian mother with several children, one of whom he accommodated on his knee. Arriving at the airport he offered the lady to carry the small child into the reception building and was first down the gangway with the child on one arm and a rucksack on the other. At the foot of the steps was a crowd of photographers and reporters. After three weeks in the Camargue sunshine he was as brown as any Algerian so the photographers asked him to pose and the reporters asked him numerous questions about conditions in Algeria. Having a good command of French and a vivid imagination he did not disappoint them but I fear that the local radio and newspapers must have given their listeners and readers a somewhat hilarious picture of the closing days in the loss of this French colony.

Bee Eater

CHAPTER SEVEN

The Land of the Lapps

We sailed from the Tyne one evening in early June on board
M.V. *Braemar* bound for Oslo and encountered rough weather.
There were three of us, George, Alan and myself on the trail of
the White-tailed Eagle, which we had failed to film in Iceland and
which had not then been re-introduced into Scotland. Its main
breeding area is the rocky coast and islands of the Finnmark
province of Norway and we had good hope of success. We had
ascertained that no official permit is needed to photograph and
film wildlife in Norway but it is all protected under the Norwegian
Hunting Act 1952 which says 'it is not allowed to disturb birds'
nests.'

Nearly all of the land in Finnmark is owned by the State, on
which no permission is needed to enter but we did inform the
Public Owner in Vadsø of our intended visit and activity. We
procured a copy of the booklet published by the Norwegian State
Game Research Institute which sets out all the rules for game
management, so that we would not offend any of them.

We docked in Oslo thirty-eight hours later, where we were met
by my friend Meidell at 06.00 hours and he helped us with the
formalities of putting our Landrover on the road. This was
essential to our expedition, being equipped for snow and off-the-
road travel besides being fitted with sleeping and eating facilities
and, most important, mosquito-proof screens.

We followed Meidell's car to his home on the outskirts of Oslo
where we enjoyed typical Norwegian hospitality at an excellent
breakfast. We spent the day seeing some of the many interesting
sights of Oslo and the evening in telephoning contacts further
north for news of breeding sites of the White-tailed Eagle,
sometimes named in English the Sea Eagle, in Norwegian
Havørn, and having the scientific name of *Haliaetus albicilla*,
which latter we used when speaking by telephone to ornitholog-

ists to avoid any possibility of error.

The highway to the far North is 2,000 miles long and our ultimate destination was Storr Ekeroy in Varangerfjord but we planned to deviate from it wherever our maps or local knowledge suggested a likely site for an eagle eyrie in occupation of a breeding pair. We left at 08.00 on the following morning, drove by Hamar and camped for the night near Trondheim. We had there a good view of a cock Willow Grouse among birch scrub but it flew before we could photograph it. This is a colourful bird with reddish brown back, white wings and black tail. It looks like the Ptarmigan but its habitat is very different. Its behaviour and flight are like that of our Red Grouse.

Next day we drove on to Rana, taking turns at the wheel. Somewhere between Krokstrand and Storjord we crossed into the Arctic Circle at 66° 32′ but saw no sign to mark it. On the third day of driving we crossed by one ferry from Bonasjirn to Skarberjit and by another to Sandwik. On every side the scenery was magnificent with spectacular waterfalls by the roadside and snowcapped mountains in the distance. On the next day we stopped at Skjoinen Fjord where we visited the Research Station and also examined prehistoric carvings.

We had a mission to fulfil in Narvik: a friend in England, who travels much in Norway, had asked us to leave 12 kgs of sugar at an address he gave us. I think he had run short of sugar on some previous journey and wished to repay what he borrowed. We eventually found the street and the block of flats but could raise no response to our knocking and ringing so we just had to leave this large package of sugar at the door of the flat and hope it reached him safely. We heard no more from the donor or recipient. Narvik was often in the news during World War II, whence the Germans used to ship iron ore until the British Navy blockaded it; it was all very peaceful as we passed through it.

We had to take a ferry across Lyngenfjord but found the pier at Lyngen under repair and so returned to the winter pier at Furuflatn, whence the ferry crossed to Olderdalen. These ferries which cross the western fjords save many miles of travel and carry a miscellaneous cargo of animals and vehicles. We camped overnight on a pleasant site between the road and the sea on the edge of a marshy area which looked interesting. We found Phalarope there and eventually located the nest well hidden amongst reeds. These were the Red-necked Phalarope and, as usual with this species, the cock bird was incubating. The light was not very good for filming and as I moved around in the marsh and stood awhile in a wet patch I was unaware that I was sinking to my knees. When I did try to move, I found both feet stuck fast. After a good laugh and a few photographs being taken of my plight I pulled my feet out of my wellies and was rescued by my two companions forming a chain to drier land. The wellies were rescued later by a similar operation.

We entered Finnmark between Stokkedalen and Breidalen and I was reminded how this whole area was laid waste by the German occupying forces as they abandoned it, houses and huts were burned, and the sparse population was herded onto coastal vessels to be landed in southern Norway. I was in Oslo in 1946 where I called upon the Department for the Rehabilitation of Finnmark. As I entered an office a tall and elderly Norwegian was leaving. My friend there told me about his interview; he wanted permission to return to his village in Finnmark. The man was over sixty years of age.

'But how will you travel if you do get a permit?' the official asked. 'there is no transport of any kind'. 'I shall walk, it's not much more than 1,600 kilometres.' 'And what will you do when you arrive? There are no buildings or electricity or crops. It has been laid waste.' 'O, I shall take my saw and hammer. I shall manage with them.'

He did not receive his permit to return so soon but my friend admired his typical courage and hardihood.

Happily, all the devastation has now been made good. Indeed, the village with brightly painted wooden houses looked prosperous, the people as always cheerful and kindly, and the environment immaculate. Many fence posts in a village were topped by a fishbox in which Herring Gulls made their nests. These were placed so that the owner could collect the eggs, which are quite good to eat, though somewhat fishy to taste. So long as

Red-throated
Phalarope

eggs are taken, leaving one or two in the nest, the Gull will continue to lay during the breeding season.

In the tiny ports there were great wooden racks for drying fish and these were well filled with cod and herring. They became a familiar part of the landscape.

We had made contact by telephone from Oslo with a man who knew of an Eagles' eyrie not far from his home. We called upon him and, although he could not accompany us, he gave us detailed directions how we should find it. There could be no near approach by road but we could take our vehicles to a boathouse on the opposite shore of the fjord. Within we should find several boats with outboard motors. We would recognise his by a painting on the bows. He could not remember the English name of his painted mascot but with much hilarity and attempted sketching it turned out to be Mickey Mouse!

Eventually we found the boathouse and the boat and his spare can of petrol. We sailed up and down the opposite shore of the fjord, scanning every likely ledge but we could find no sign of the White-tailed Eagle's eyrie, nor any sight of an eagle. We landed on a small jetty and followed a path which led to a youth hut where we talked to a caretaker. He knew nothing of eagles in the area but he did tell us of a lynx having been shot under the hut a few weeks earlier. And so we returned the way we had come and tied up Mickey Mouse and left a note to thank our friend for his generous help.

The Arctic Circle marks the division of the Frigid Zone from the Temperate Zone. Its fascination for bird watchers lies not only in the indigenous birds like the Snowy Owl but also in the birds of passage which fly north from southern Europe, from the Mediterranean, from North and Central and even South Africa to breed in the high north. The urge to keep flying north to the limit of the land mass must be to facilitate breeding and the raising of young. There are twenty-four hours of daylight instead of twelve on the Equator. There is abundant food supply, especially for the insectivorous species; there is less pressure of competition for food and nesting sites and less predation.

The breeding season is very short – a mere ten weeks but some

Ruffs display

species manage to raise two broods in this short time. The means they adopt to achieve this are very interesting. The Sanderling has two nests and two broods concurrently, the female incubating and feeding one and the male the other. Temmink's Stint also has multiple broods but for this species the first nest is made – a mere scrape on the ground – the clutch of eggs laid and abandoned whilst the second nest is prepared by both parents, the hen is fertilised and a second clutch is laid. The cock bird then returns to incubate and feed the first clutch. The two nests may be quite widely separated. In other species the female is unashamedly polygamous and the male birds are left to do all the incubating and rearing. It is noticeable that the eggs of these multiple breeders are relatively smaller in relation to bodyweight so that the demand on the metabolism of the hen is not too great in producing twice the number of eggs usual for waders.

As we went north the conifer trees grew progressively shorter until at Skaldt the road divides, west to Hammerfest and east to Vadsø. We turned east to skirt the southern shore of Varanger fjord where we camped for the night and watched Golden Plover, Common Scoter and Scaup on the water. In the morning we filmed the Red-necked Phalarope with the usual difficulty of keeping the birds far enough away from our feet to remain in focus. After a short run we stopped to film another waterfall – Adamfoss. There had been so many beautiful waterfalls on our route that we had become quite blasé about them and scarcely stopped to admire them. But Adamfoss is so spectacular that we had to gaze in admiration and attempt to capture its beauty on film. At Lakselv we watched two male Goosanders fishing. They were methodically trawling the water and, although they caught nothing as we watched, they do catch a great many fish when feeding young and they are not popular with fishermen.

We reached Vadsø at 15.30 hours, having travelled by road 1,565 English miles since leaving Oslo. We were beyond the tree line and in the tundra zone. We skirted the northern shore of Varangerfjord to Vardø where we were on almost the same latitude as the North Cape and over 300 English miles within the Arctic Circle. With the sun high in the heavens it was quite warm

Turnstone

but as the sun dipped toward the horizon – but never below it – the cold was intense.

Vadsø looked very clean and prosperous. The wooden houses all seemed new and were gaily painted. The few cars about the street all looked new. The roads are in excellent condition. It was here we saw Ruffs and Reeves in full breeding plumage and in considerable numbers in the fields and among the heather. The ruffs or mantles of the cock birds were in a variety of colours – black, white, cream, chestnut and dark purple. The male stood very erect and tall like a game bird, his back plumage was mottled brown but cream on the belly and chin. His slightly curved bill was flesh coloured, as were also his long legs, which stepped boldly and proudly over the heather, totally unafraid.

The ornamental ruffs and the ear tufts of the cocks were erected most of the time, Reeves being in the vicinity and other cock birds strutting in their own jousting yards, but I saw no fights. With head held high the Ruffs peered out of their mantles like a woman peering out of an expensive fur cape, as if conscious of the effect of such splendour on the observers. I noticed that, when he did lower the mantle, it parted at the back into two halves which he brought forwards and down.

Standing by the shore of a small peninsular that ran out into the fjord, I watched fascinated from one spot Red-necked Phalarope, Temmink's Stint, Ringed Plover, Turnstone, Dunlin, Oyster-catcher, Eider Duck, Longtail Duck, and Arctic Tern, all going about their affairs and apparently ignoring the intrusion of three humans. No hides were needed to film birds on the nest.

One Temmink's Stint that we wanted to film coming onto her nest was back onto the eggs before we had erected the tripod. She seemed to have no fear of us at all but only regarded us as rather a nuisance. Both the Temmink's Stint and the Little Stint were present but it was not easy to distinguish between these two tiny waders except at close quarters, when the legs of the former were seen to be black and of the latter green. However, it appeared to us that Temmink's frequented the sea shore whilst the Little Stint was found further inland amongst vegetation at the edge of pools and marshes. Both species utter a pleasing trill.

After some days of rain we enjoyed beautiful and continuous sunshine. We filmed Goosanders, Mergansers and Scoters on the water and Turnstone and Bar-tailed Godwit on the shore. On one occasion we watched a flock of twenty-five Bar-tailed Godwits feeding on the shore-line. On a still evening with the tide ebbing the shore-line was alive with birds feeding – Dunlin and Redshank, Oystercatcher and Turnstone. Stooping to the water, the beautiful Arctic Tern reminded us of home, for they breed on the Farne Islands. On the water were the familiar Eider drakes and one day a flotilla of Steller's Eider came past us close inshore.

As the sun sank towards the horizon we became more conscious of the wealth of sound, the lapping waves and the variety of bird calls – the deep 'urrch' of the Eider, the shrill piping of the Oystercatcher, the musical note of the Redshank (which is arguably the loveliest sound in nature), the quick repetitive whistle of the Turnstone, and the four musical notes of the Long-tailed Duck. We had a splendid view of the Long-tail on a pond a little inland; it was the drake and he swam in circles whilst we filmed him. His mate was not in view but doubtless crouching on her eggs in a nest well hidden on the island. We used a lot of film on him because he is a rarity for us, not breeding in Britain and usually at sea when not breeding. His appearance is striking, being boldly patterned in white and dark brown with a long and slender drooping tail.

Another rarity we were lucky to see was the Smew. Half a dozen of these beautiful little saw-bill ducks swam past us close inshore. In the water it looks pure white with a black eye-patch and a small crest. Unfortunately we had no cameras to hand and we never saw them again. They breed only in the high North of Norway and we missed a wonderful opportunity.

With all these rare and splendid birds to watch and film we had not forgotten our main objective, the White-tailed Eagle. We looked and enquired everywhere we went. It was not until the second week that we saw one flying at a distance. On the following day as we drove along the coast road we came upon one suddenly when we turned a corner. No chance to film or photograph! We just sat and stared. It was an adult male standing

Ruff

Kittiwakes

on an outcrop of rock on the roadside. He was tremendously impressive, pale brown in colour with a great hooked bill of vivid yellow. He looked at us disdainfully and then launched into the air, displaying his prominent wedge-shaped white tail! As he flapped leisurely away, the great span of his dark wings lifting him to soaring height. We watched him disappear, determined to find his eyrie wherever it might be.

Next day we forced a passage along a snow-bound road to Hammingberg which is the end of the coast road. Here lived a man, Erling, who could tell us the whereabouts of the eyrie, though it might well be on an inaccessible island. Although it was mid-June, the road was drifted deep with snow and we received a great welcome when we reached the little fishing village. We understood that ours was the first wheeled vehicle to reach them since the onset of winter but they had good radio communication with Vadsø and could, of course, be reached by boat or by sledge if the sea was frozen. Our welcome included a fine meal at which a celebration cake was cut in our honour. Unfortunately Erling did not know of any eyrie but urged us to take a boat to a bird cliff at Styllingfjord where, he said, White-tailed Eagles were often seen but there was no eyrie. However, he said, it was well worth a visit for, thousands of sea birds nest on the sheer cliffs – Kittiwakes, Puffins, Guillemots, Black Guillemots, Little Auks and Gannets. We did not accept his kind invitation to take us because all these sea birds, except the Little Auk, breed also in the British Isles and we can see the Little Auk there also in winter so we did not think it worth spending a whole day on the sea-trip.

That evening we decided to camp on the shore of the Arctic Ocean instead of returning to Varangerfjord and our usual camp site. As the sun sank it became cold and we thought how comforting would be a roaring fire to sit beside as we ate our supper but, of course, there were no trees to provide wood, nor any heather. Without much hope we searched the shore for flotsam and to our surprise, we found quantities of wood planks, crates, and other timber thrown up by the waves onto the stony beach. I suppose that passing ships' crews throw everything they do not want overboard, as is the practice of sailors the world over, and it all ends up on the northern shores of Europe, Siberia and the island north of Canada. We were grateful for their untidy habits and had a glorious fire which kept us out of our chilly beds until the early hours of morning.

We met an Englishman one day, whom we knew vaguely, and stopped his Range Rover to talk with him. He had two German men in the car with him whom he was shepherding around Lapland, and whom he introduced to us. We asked if they were ornithologists. No, no, – just interested in wildlife generally. We would have enjoyed a longer discussion with the Englishman, whom we knew to be keen on birds and knowledgeable about the high North, but the Germans were impatient to be on their way. He told us where their tents were pitched and we promised to call on them to exchange news at a more convenient time. Two days later we did visit them as their two tents were only 100 metres off the road. Their vehicle was not there and the tents were laced up. We succumbed to curiosity and peeped inside. To our horror one of the tents was lined with egg boxes. This explained the reluctance of the two Germans to talk because any egg-collecting in Norway is illegal. And they were doing this on a big scale. I reported the incident later by letter to *Directoratet For Jakt, Viltstell Og Ferskvannis Fiske*; they replied that they were aware of the depredations of egg-thefts on a commercial scale but the area is so vast that they could not provide wardens to protect it all. We never saw these three men again.

The basis of the Lapp economy is the reindeer and some Lapps are alleged to be very wealthy by ownership of vast herds. We watched them flowing over the hillside in hundreds as they moved to new feeding grounds. Their owners follow the herd's migration to and from their breeding area and in their constant search for the lichen on which they feed. They are culled in the late summer by selected beasts being driven into a stockade when they are lassoed and their throats cut. We did not witness this massacre which must be a grim though necessary operation but we were told that every bit of each slaughtered beast is used or sold, so nothing is wasted. The trend towards increased tourism in the high North makes one wonder how long this culture dependent on semi-wild animals will endure.

We were invited to meet a Lapp lady described as the 'Queen of the Lapps' – Fru Smuk, who lived at Vadsø – and who allegedly owned the largest herd. We accepted this in expectation of learning about reindeer management; we thought we should see inside a Lapp tent of reindeer hide or, at least, a Norwegian wooden hut. But in the event her home proved to be a modern brick-built house and we learned very little about reindeer movement but more about the advantages of mechanised transport. Fru Smuk was small of stature, like all Lapps, and of an indeterminate age. Her features were Mongolian and her skin dark. She spoke Lappish but had some Norwegian. As her knowledge of that language was little better than my smattering, our conversation was difficult and we did not stay long.

We explored the southern shore of Varangerfjord through the village of Gandvik to Kirkenes. Not wishing to cross the border into USSR, we returned by the same road to Varangerbotn, where we turned south into Finland. We had watched Lapland Buntings on the shore but nothing else that was new. No passports were examined at the border and no customs formalities. It would have been different had we crossed into USSR! We stopped on the road to Ivalo to walk up onto a snow-covered hillside where we expected to find Dotterel but found none. But we did have a splendid view of an arctic fox hunting; he had moulted his white coat and his rusty fur stood out vividly against the snow. We watched him through field glasses at distances varying from a half to one and a half kilometres and he ignored us completely. His tracks showed clearly in the snow; they zig-zagged over the whole moor within our view; his hunting did not appear to follow any plan; he was probably trying to pick up the scent of Ptarmigan or lemming.

On our return to the car we did see a single lemming which form a basic food source for the arctic fox, Snowy Owl, and other predators. Their numbers vary enormously from year to year and in peak years the winged predators gather to take a huge toll which does keep their numbers under control for they breed three times a year, starting under the snow, and the gestation

Bluethroat

period is only three weeks. The first brood start to breed at the end of the short summer so the population can explode if there is plenty of vegetation to eat. It is this explosion which causes the migration of lemmings to find better feeding grounds. The popular idea of mass suicide to save the whole race from starvation is probably a romantic fiction.

We skirted a big lake on which Common Scoters were evidently breeding and we watched Golden Plover with which we are familiar on our moors at home. This was, of course, the northern form with black face, breast and belly and a white stripe running round the eye, down the side of the neck to the rump and tail. The back and wing coverts are richly spotted with gold. When we reached the tree line of dwarf birch we were rewarded with sightings of the Arctic Redpoll with its vivid red crown and white rump. Our Redpoll at home is a common bird of about the same size but with brighter pink on the breast and a streaked rump.

Our next night's stay was planned to be near Rovaniemi where George had some friends he wished to visit but as we entered the more thickly forested country of spruce trees we stopped to look for the Red-spotted Bluethroat which is a bird of the conifer forests with a habit of flirting the tail like our Redstart. We had only a fleeting view of a male bird amongst the dense foliage and no chance to film it. Our lack of patience was largely due to mosquitoes. They looked to be as large as honey bees and as ferocious as killer bees. It is odd how one's experience with rats and mosquitoes always assumes that they are bigger than anyone else has ever experienced.

We travelled until we sighted a wayside stall with racks of reindeer horns, fur hats and other souvenirs. We thought it a good plan to buy presents here to take home to our families rather than in Oslo, as the prices would be more reasonable. A very pretty girl was in charge, dressed in Lapp national costume but obviously not a Lapp; she was tall, fair-haired, and with good features. Trade had not been brisk; we were probably her first, and perhaps only, customers that day so there was no urgency to make our selection. We held a stilted conversation in her Swedish and my few words of Norwegian, which at least gave us the prices of her goods in Finmarks, and they were reasonable. The mosquitoes gathered for a further onslaught but the girl was quite immune. Before he could complete any purchase Alan's nerve broke and he ran for cover into the Landrover where the fly screen protected him from attack. George and I stuck it out until we had bought some antlers and fur hats but we suffered severe swellings on necks and wrists.

As we neared Rovaniemi we saw an attractive camp site and decided we should obey the local rules to camp in designated sites rather than in the wilds, as is our wont. It proved to be well organised with sanitation, water supply, a shop and a restaurant; we made good use of the facilities at modest cost and there were few other campers. George telephoned his friends who invited us to breakfast on the following morning at a time which seemed to us more appropriate for a mid-day meal – 10.00 a.m. We looked around the town and visited a natural history museum to fill in the time between our two breakfasts. The museum of mounted specimens of local birds was small but nicely displayed which enabled us to check some of our earlier identifications in the field.

We were made welcome to the home of Mr and Mrs Inaison, whose English was fluent, so conversation presented no problem.

After a decent interval and before Finnish hospitality could press us to stay to lunch we set off to travel south to cross the border into Sweden at Tornio which lies at the very head of the Baltic. Once again formalities scarcely existed and we took the western road to Haparanda and thence to Lulea and south towards Sundsval. But we decided to turn off at Kramfors to go due west through Ostersund and cross the Norwegian border near Trondheim. We camped before we reached the border, having just pulled off the road. We watched badgers as they emerged from their set in the gloaming before we turned in. As we prepared breakfast in the morning there was a Woodcock probing its long bill into soft earth nearby, a Pied Wagtail feeding young, and a Redwing with a nest in a nearby bush.

Next day we drove through Trondheim and took the right fork. As we had sufficient time before embarking in Oslo, we decided to drive through the high mountain area of Jotunheimen and to camp in Bøverdal. In an open space amongst trees we had a splendid view of an elk; it was an adult male and it ran like a horse, seemingly at a loss to know which way to run. It was difficult to judge its size at a distance but it appeared to me to approximate to the size and build of a 16 hands horse.

There was an authorised camping site near Spiterstulen with wooden huts attractively spaced out amongst the trees and we decided to use this rather than risk offending some landowner. Moreover we wanted a base from which to explore this beautiful countryside and to study the bird life in it. By backing our Landrover up to the open door of our chosen hut, we had the comfort and privacy of both. In our walks that evening and the following morning we saw many familiar birds – Redstart, Willow Warbler, Whinchat, Redwing, Fieldfare, Magpie and Hooded Crow. This last is a sub-species of the Carrion Crow and is very like it in size and habits; but it is grey on the back and belly instead of being all black. We see it in the north and west of Scotland where it may inter-breed with the Carrion Crow but it is endemic throughout Scandinavia. We watched also Wheatears in summer plumage. Six species of Wheatear are known in Europe but here was *Oenanthe oenanthe*, the best known. All have the significant white rump which is very conspicuous and gives them their name.

The cock bird in his spring plumage is very handsome in his dress of black, white and grey with a pinkish buff breast.

We drove to Olden and thence walked up to the foot of the Briksdal glacier which is a splendid sight of green, blue and white ice caves where it ends in a pool and a river of ice-cold water. At Stryn there were many young people skiing on the high ground and it was good to watch them enjoying themselves on powdery snow and wearing a minimum of brightly coloured clothing in the warm sunshine.

On another day, we took the car to the village of Spiterstulen which is a tourist attraction because of the ancient wooden huts which are still in use. I decided to walk back to the camp, being all downhill, and to have a better view of the deep gorge on one side of the road. Bramblings, Redstarts, and Greenfinches were much in evidence. Only on foot was it possible to appreciate the magnificence of the scenery. On my left as I descended the rough road was the deep gorge cut by the glacier a few thousand years ago and now deepened by the rushing torrent. I turned aside frequently through the few metres of forest to reach its edge. In one place I saw a great rock projecting out over the cliff and there I stopped to admire the views it provided both up and down the valley. Nine hundred metres beneath me the river raced between granite walls in a tumult of white water. Many small waterfalls leaped into the abyss from the far side or fell like white lace draped over the dark rock.

With the warmth of the sun and the sound of the water I felt sleepy, pulled off my shirt to feel the caress of the sun, and lay back on the bare granite. Almost at once I fell asleep and began to dream. There was a girl beside me of surpassing beauty; the tendrils of her honey-coloured hair were blowing in the wind against the richer gold of her sun-warmed skin.

Awed by the majesty of our precarious perch, I whispered, 'We are eagles here, ready to soar on eddying currents of the wind into the rarer atmosphere to look upon the curvature of earth and to watch men struggling like ants.'

'Eagles today,' she agreed, 'but tomorrow lemmings, earth-bound and temporal. Let us remember this moment of glory through the deepening gloom.'

The air was sweet with the resin of spruce trees and we spoke above the song of falling water. Her beauty focused the warm sun like a burning-glass upon my brain which burst into sudden flame so that I reached out both my hands towards her with a rush of hot words in my throat. But, 'Do not say it,' she urged, her eyes deep wells of tenderness. 'What you would say is better left unsaid. It can never be for us.'

She leaned forward to look down into the dizzy depths below and her blowing hair caressed my face. The sweetness of her was like the harvesting of new-mown hay.

'This for remembrance,' she said and, turning swiftly, kissed me full upon the mouth. 'Remember this one day and keep it as an ordinance for ever.'

On that instant I awoke to find myself alone upon the rock and too near the edge for safety. The sun was lower now and the heat had gone out of it; I scrambled to my feet and pulled on my shirt. My friends would think I was lost so I hastened on my way.

On the following morning we broke camp and motored uneventfully to Oslo. In the home of our Norwegian friends I picked up an evening paper and there on the front page was the picture of a girl: it was the girl upon the rock. Although in black and white, it was the same girl; no doubt of it. I tried to understand the significance of the typescript below the photograph but could make out only *'Tilfelle'* which I knew could mean 'accident'.

'What does it say?' I asked my friend. 'Oh, it's the report of a car accident yesterday. This girl was killed in Jotunheimen. Why? Do you know her?' I mumbled something about a resemblance to someone I knew and we spoke no more about it. That evening we saw our Landrover loaded onto the ship and our Norwegian saga was over.

CHAPTER EIGHT

The Sunset Isles

The road to the Hebrides for George and me went by Fort William to the Kyle of Lochalsh and thence to Skye, where we spent a day to look at scenery and people and birds. We were there earlier in the year than the great throng of tourists so the roads were relatively quiet; we turned westward off the main road to Torrin and beyond to have a clear view of the high peaks of the Cuillins – Bahachdich and Sgurr Diargi and Sgurr Alasdair – red rock of primitive creation, awesome to regard, treacherous to climb.

I saw my first Twite and we found the nest with four eggs in it; it is an undistinguished rufous coloured finch, the male having a rose coloured rump and a pale yellow bill. The female sitting on her nest was less colourful. The nest was on a rocky ledge amongst heather. Later we saw many of this species which we do not find commonly in England.

Two hundred years ago Boswell described in his *Tour to the Hebrides* the cottages in Skye as single storey with low walls and no windows, 'the walls often formed by two exterior surfaces of stone, filled up with earth in the middle, which makes them very warm. The roof is generally bad. They are thatched with straw, sometimes with heath, sometimes with fern. The thatch is secured with ropes of straw or heath, and, to fix the ropes, there is a stone tied to the end of each. I should think, when there is wind, they would come down and knock people on the head.'

We saw no such cottages as we motored the length of Skye; indeed, the houses were modern and well maintained, indicating a high standard of prosperity. But we did see many cottages in Uist, which fitted Boswell's description aptly; however, it seemed that these were being used for storage and no longer as dwellings.

Samuel Johnson and he did not reach Uist in their famous tour but they did venture so far as the small islands such as Ulva,

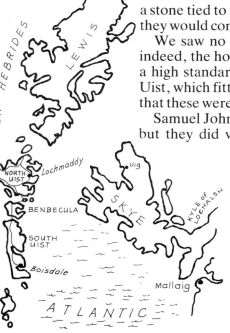

necessitating journeys on horseback and in open rowing boats, often in atrocious weather. I think Dr Johnson was aged about sixty years at the time; he must have been tougher than he looks in the usual portrait we see of him, for they were obliged sometimes to spend the night on a pile of hay in a barn and suffered many discomforts.

We were more fortunate for we travelled easily on good roads north to Uig harbour, from whence we took a ferry in the evening to Lochmaddy on North Uist. We stopped often on the road to watch familiar birds and especially a cock Stonechat in his splendid spring livery on the top of a dry stone wall. In the bright sunshine his black head, white collar, and rusty-red breast looked extremely smart.

Another bird we watched by the roadside was a Cornbunting which was uttering what passes for a song as it perched on a wire fence. It flew off with its legs dangling, which is one of its peculiarities.

Having arrived at Uig Pier too early for the ferry, we went to the top of a high cliff to watch the Fulmars performing aerial acrobatics on the upward currents of wind with amazing virtuosity. They could hang on the air with scarcely a wing movement and our position on the cliff top enabled us to study them without glasses at only two or three metres distance. They were nesting on the ledges beneath us with only a scrape in the vegetation or among loose stones to serve as a refuge for the single dirty-white egg. The powerful yellow bill was hooked at the extremity of the upper mandible which bore the large tubular nostrils typical of its genus. From our vantage point we could admire the pearly grey of the mantle of the sitting birds.

We did not linger at Lochmaddy in North Uist but motored directly to its southern tip, crossed the causeway to Benbecula and the other causeway to South Uist, and so to Boisdale at the southern end of South Uist, where we had arranged to stay for a few days in the home of a friend of George, who made us welcome. We intended to see Loch Hallan and the birds of North Uist in better light.

Our first objective next morning was to set up our hides at four

Fulmars

Stonechat

chosen nests on the Machair, which is the word used to describe the common land between the high tide line and the cultivated fields. This sandy strip is sparsely covered with vegetation and is much favoured by a variety of gulls and waders as a nesting site. We had no problem in locating several nests of the Oystercatcher, Lapwing, and Golden Plover. The Dunlin nests were easy to find too because they chose the tufts of taller grass, of which there were few. It took longer to pin-point the nest of a pair of Ringed Plovers, which we knew was there because of the parents flying around but refusing to come to the nest whilst we were watching. We had to retire to our car parked at two hundred metres distance and watch them continuously through field glasses before we could see the hen bird go to the nest and incubate the eggs which are wonderfully camouflaged and the nest no more than a scrape in the sand. This unremitting stare through powerful glasses at an almost invisible object for about twenty minutes so strained my eyes that I suffered a violent headache that night. But our subsequent film of this lovely little wader was worth it.

Staying in the same house was a young science graduate engaged upon a project which had a strictly limited allocation of time and money. We saw him only briefly at our early breakfast and again briefly in the evening for he had fallen in love with a local girl and always changed his working clothes and hurried to meet her as soon as his work was done. But he had a Landrover and we a saloon car which was unsuitable for crossing rough ground and carrying hides from one site to another. George persuaded him that his girl friend would be more favourably impressed by a smart saloon car than a Landrover and arranged an exchange for the day. Every morning over porridge and ham and eggs this comedy was enacted and every time he fell for our persuasion and we borrowed the more suitable vehicle. And every second evening he telephoned his superior in Edinburgh to prolong his stay on the island for a few more days to complete his project. We knew what that project really was but we left before he did and never learned whether our car persuaded her to marry him.

We turned our attention to Loch Boisdale where we filmed

Redshanks on the shore and, the Common Gull nesting among thick grass in an adjacent field. There were several nests of this species which is like a smaller edition of the Herring Gull but the bill and legs have a green tinge; it is not nearly so common as the Herring Gull despite its name and I suppose this indicates the change in population of these two species, the latter being ubiquitous round the coast of Great Britain and the Common breeding only in Northern Ireland, Northern Scotland and the Islands in U.K. The parent came very readily to our chosen nest and proved an ideal subject to film.

We had heard Corncrakes in the early hours of the morning near to our lodging and we traced this sound to a large patch of nettles near a farmhouse. Sure enough we found an obvious path trodden through the nettles but could see no nest. We forbore to tread amongst them lest we should disturb a nesting bird; although we waited patiently for long periods at a distance hoping to see the bird come into or out of the nettle patch, we never had sight of it. This secretive bird is a summer visitor to the west of England, Scotland and Northern Ireland. It is crepuscular in habit and its presence is made known by the rasping and repetitive voice of the male during the breeding season. Half a century ago it was quite common in its chosen areas but the numbers have continuously dwindled in England; the Western Isles seem to be its last refuge. We were disappointed not to see it but glad we had not disturbed it.

A gamekeeper told us where we might see the eyrie of a pair of Golden Eagles in the hills in the interior of the island and we duly located it. Unfortunately it had not been used this year; eagles have three or four favoured nest sites which they use in rotation. But we did see this magnificent bird soaring high above us and we clambered down to the rocky ledge to see the old nest measuring about a metre and a half across and some bones of hares and game birds around it. We knew of another eyrie in North Uist that we planned to visit. On our return we called again at the gamekeeper's house to tell him the situation and he consoled us with a tumbler of neat whisky, which he described as a 'wee dram'. I do not know whether it was the product of an illicit

Golden Eagle

distillery, but it tasted good.

These island folk have life very well organised and, though regarded as being 'disadvantaged' they know how to take advantage of every kind of grant and subsidy. I had remarked how many of the fields were surrounded by new wire fences with the old fences left standing alongside them. I was informed that the subsidy of a new fence was greater than the cost of repairing an old fence. I also learned that a grant was made to any young woman attending an old lady who was a neighbour but not if it was her mother; so daughter A looked after B's mother and vice versa and each received a grant. Maybe this ruse was perpetrated elsewhere in U.K. but I never heard of it. If there was any legitimate way to augment their hard-earned income, these people found it.

We hired a small boat and rowed out to the fishers' islands lying a short distance from the harbour, where we knew Herons were nesting. Instead of being built at the very top of tall trees, where we usually find a heronry located, these nests were less than a metre above ground on top of low gorse bushes. As we landed on the rocks the few adults on the island took off with heavily flapping wings and the ugly youngsters in the bulky nests of sticks showed no particular concern at our presence. As there are few tall trees on Uist, I suppose the Herons found the surrounding water gave them ample protection from predators. We took a number of still photographs but it was obvious that the parents would not bring food to the young ones so long as we were in sight and there was no cover on the island.

We rowed back to the harbour, observing both Great Black-backed and Lesser Black-backed Gulls on the way. Apart from size, they may be differentiated by the colour of the legs, but both species are predators and scavengers and thieves of other sea-birds' eggs. We saw a Little Tern which is easily identified by its small size and confirmed by the white forehead under the black crown and then a black eye-stripe. The bill and legs are yellow.

When returning the boat and paying for its hire we learned that there had been pandemonium in the harbour after our departure. It is customary for all visitors and some of the residents to park

Red-throated Diver

their cars overnight on the quays. To lock the cars' doors or to remove ignition keys would be resented by the inhabitants as a reflection on their honesty. But when the owners went to pick up their cars that morning, none of the ignition keys would start the engines. If they were in the keyholes they would not turn and if they were not, they were on the driver's seat and would not enter the keyholes. Frantic owners found that the keys of twenty-three cars had all been changed around. The permutations were such that it took an hour for every owner to find his own key; the last car to have its rightful key returned was our own because we had had no need of it. The author of this terrible trick was eventually found to be the son of our hosts. After leaving home for school that morning he had meticulously changed the keys of all the cars. He was an only child, spoiled by his mother and the despair of his father.

Loch Hallan is a nature reserve; we went there to study the Grey Lag Geese which breed socially on the marshy ground surrounding it. We did not enter the reserve for fear of disturbing the nesting birds for great efforts are made to encourage these geese which do not migrate north in the breeding season to breed successfully in Britain. This was the West European race of the Grey Lag with an orange-coloured bill without any black marks on it.

The grey geese have to be examined in detail with binoculars to distinguish between them as the distinctive features are mainly the legs and bills and any white markings on the head, of which the Grey Lag and the Pink-footed have none. The name of the Grey Lag is said to be derived from the tendency of some of this species wintering with us and being fed by farmers to attempt to domesticate them to lag behind when the main skein sets off on its annual migration to breeding grounds in the far north. Also on the Loch we saw a Red-throated Diver followed by a single juvenile, a Dabchick with her young on her back, and a pair of Mute Swans. Swallows were darting above it, making a lovely picture.

We crossed over Benbecula to reach North Uist where we planned to visit another well-known Golden Eagle eyrie and we

Grey-lag Geese

found it without difficulty. We could not film this because we had no permit and we had anyhow insufficient time to build a hide of local materials progressively over a number of days. This eyrie was high on a cliff face with only one possible ledge on which a hide could be located. This meant that one of our standard canvas hides could not be placed at a safe distance and moved gradually nearer to the nest. The strategy then must be to build a hide of rock and heather by stages so that the birds are not alarmed by the sudden appearance of a new structure.

There was a single eaglet in the nest which we could clearly see through binoculars but a parent might only come once during the day with food and an observer must be prepared to wait many hours each day over a period of several days to obtain a good view or worthwhile photographs. We waited for two hours when the male bird did fly into view. It had no prey in its talons and so was not coming to the nest. We could see clearly the golden sheen on the feathers of its head and nape which give it its name. It chased off a Hen Harrier which was patrolling up and down the valley searching for food. This was the male, a lovely soft grey in colour with a white patch on the rump and black tips to the wings.

On our return to Boisdale we saw three Short-eared Owls, a pair of Ravens, and a Hoodie Crow. Altogether it was a good day to complete a very rewarding week in these Western Isles.

CHAPTER NINE

Our Oldest Ally

Portugal is the only country in Europe in which the Black-winged Kite is known to breed; this became known quite recently and even there it is a rarity. This inspired us to mount an expedition to film it, which had not hitherto been achieved to our knowledge, although it is not uncommon throughout Africa under the name of the Black-shouldered Kite, which is a more accurate description. We hoped also to find the Great Bustard, which still breeds in the southern plains of Portugal and Spain, though no longer on the South Downs of England, where once it was indigenous.

Taking turns to drive our specially equipped Landrover, George, Harvey and I travelled from County Durham to the outskirts of Bordeaux nonstop except on the Dover/Calais ferry. We suffered a delay when the French customs officials waved us to one side when we disembarked our vehicle which appeared to interest them more than the routine tourist car. Certainly it merited inspection, being loaded to the roof with camping gear and food, cameras and sound-recording equipment, and a dismantled bird hide. Eventually we were on our way, having satisfied them that we carried no arms or drugs or contraband, but were apparently harmless idiots.

We took a few hours' sleep in a wood off the roadside in the early hours of the morning and then stopped in Biarritz to buy some long French loaves. We crossed the frontier to San Sebastian where the Spanish Customs proved to be even more officious than the French. Because the Black-winged Kites nest in tall trees we had made preparation to film them at the nest by having made a special tower of aluminium tubes with a platform eight metres from the ground, on which we could erect a canvas hide. This tower could be quickly built from two-metre tubes with thumb screws and guy ropes. Stacked in our Landrover this mass

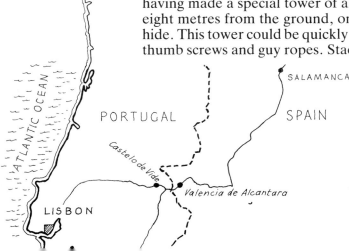

of tubes did somewhat resemble a formidable anti-aircraft missile launcher and the officials and military took some convincing that we were not planning to start a revolution. It was only when we had unloaded our carefully packed stores to the point where frying pans and stewpots began to fall to the ground was their curiosity sated. At future customs examinations we always packed these culinary utensils and a bag of apples in a position to fall out and roll about the ground as soon as we opened the rear door. This so exasperated the officials that they cut short the examination and were glad to see us go.

We drove to Vitoria, Burgos, and Salamanca, passing in the earlier stages up a steep valley with a river on our right. It was very noticeable how the river changed its character from being little better than a sewer by reason of the effluent poured into it from factories and towns near the coast to a glorious torrent as we climbed into the hills. The last town we passed through in Spain was Valencia de Alcantara and by sunset we had reached the border with Portugal where our documents we quickly cleared and the Customs officials were very pleasant. We started the descent but soon decided to camp for the night so as to enjoy the downhill run on a tortuous road to our objective, Castelo de Vide.

We were very pleased to have made that decision because the winding road led us through glorious scenery in the bright morning sunshine on a journey none of us will ever forget. The foothills resembled a rock-garden ablaze with wild flowers of every colour. They could not have been placed more effectively among the rocks if an expert landscape gardener had designed it.

We arrived early in the village of Castelo de Vide when the streets were still deserted. We had corresponded with a professor of 'Silviculter', whose son was a keen birdman and he had invited us to call upon him. With the aid of our large-scale map of the area and a Portuguese phrase book we found our way to his estate a few kilometres distant. There was a large house with an impressive gateway on one side of the road and several stone outbuildings on the other. All were deserted and no amount of knocking on the door of the house brought any response; we sat

Hoopoe

down to wait. At last a man arrived at the buildings, to whom we showed a letter we had received from the Professor but he obviously could not read it, being written in English. However, the name conveyed all he needed to know and he indicated the gate on the other side of the road. By signs he made us understand that our arrival was much too early and on my watch he showed we must wait another hour before the occupant would awake. After that interval we knocked again and loudly at the house door and this time there was much rattling of chain and removal of a stout oak beam before the heavy door swung wide to reveal an elderly woman. We showed her the letter and she led us into a small room and indicated we must wait there; she took the letter away with her to show her master.

Another long wait and at last he appeared. Although we had advised him by letter that we intended to call upon him on this day, he seemed surprised to see us. Perhaps in Portugal it is unusual to keep an appointment so exactly: perhaps we had arrived at an indecently early hour. However, he was very kind. In perfect English he told us that it was his son who was the ornithologist, his subject was trees, his son was not here but had left him with some information to pass on to us of where certain species of birds might be found. We asked him about camping and he made us welcome to camp on his estate at a place three kilometres distant where was good drinking water. We promised to keep in touch with him.

We parked our vehicle, found the water supply, and cooked a second breakfast. The estate was extensive with vineyards, olive groves and parkland; it was full of birds – Hoopoes, Bee-eaters, Golden Orioles, Turtle Doves and Shrikes. We had come to the right place!

The Woodchat Shrike was unfamiliar to us so we watched several of these very colourful birds until we located the nest of one pair in the fork of an ilex tree about four metres from the ground. To film this bird at the nest required the tower hide, which we quickly assembled at a distance from the tree and moved near over three days. When they were accustomed to us, we had a splendid view of a well made nest lined with feathers and containing seven beautiful white eggs liberally spotted with grey and brown. We found two other nests with eggs of this species but decided to limit our filming to the one which now showed no fear of our presence in the hide.

We do not see this strikingly handsome bird in Britain; it is the smallest of the European Shrikes with both sexes similar in colouring, a rich chestnut crown, white throat, breast and rump, and the rest of the feathering black except for brilliant white shoulder patches. The name is interesting because it is no close relation to the Whinchat and Stonechat and its song is a warble. I have heard it said that this species was first identified by a man who thought its cry was like that of a cat and named it the 'Wood Cat Shrike'. He died before his report was printed and a compositor thought the word 'cat' should read 'chat' and so printed it.

We spent many hours in watching both parents taking turns in incubating the precious eggs and were very sad when one day we found the nest deserted and the eggs stolen by a marauding Jay.

Another Shrike's nest we found was that of the Great Grey Shrike which was located in a very different position and which could be filmed through the window of our vehicle. The nest contained five well-fledged young and both parents were feeding them assiduously. This much larger bird is grey, black and white with a long tail and slightly hooked bill and is alike in both sexes although the male has a pink tinge to the white of the breast. The food brought to the young appeared to be large insects and we saw none impaled on thorns as is the practice of this species. The male bird flew straight in and out of the nest putting his prey directly into one of the yawning gapes; but the hen always perched on a nearby spray before entering the nest; sometimes she brought a caterpillar and sometimes a bumble bee.

There was very little cultivation but we did see one man ploughing with a single furrow wooden plough drawn by a mule. The soil appeared very thin. Most of the land around us was lowland pasture with single trees scattered around to provide an attractive landscape as of a park. Many of the trees were cork oaks – *Quercus soubra* – and we watched on more than one

Great Grey Shrike

occasion how the cork bark was stripped from them. A vertical cut was made on the main trunk and the bark then levered off in a single sheet. The stripped trees looked very naked, like a newly shorn sheep.

In Castelo de Vide we filmed a White Stork brooding three young in a clumsy nest of sticks perched on top of a domestic chimney pot; but as it remained immobile we expended little footage on it. Later we made a more interesting sequence of the same species feeding in a marshy field near the river. This huge bird is all white except for its black flight feathers; it stalked sedately with long red legs among the wet vegetation, jabbing occasionally with its great red bill at any frog or lizard in its path. It breeds in Southern Europe and winters in South Africa.

The Hoopoes in the estate where we camped would have kept us awake all night were we not so tired. The monotonous call continued throughout the hours of darkness – 'hoop-hoop-poo'. We wanted to film this species at the nest as it is only an occasional visitor to southern England. We observed the regular flight path of a pair carrying food and eventually tracked them down a hole in the stump of an ancient hollow tree. This held four fledged young in an evil-smelling nest; they thrust their heads out of the vertical hole whenever they heard a parent approach, which occurred at almost two-minute intervals. The adult always landed on the stump with its lovely crest fully erected and thrust its long curved bill into the hole. This beautiful bird is pink in colour with boldly striped black and white wings and tail and its picturesque crest is pink with black tips. Before we left the area the young had flown and we noticed that they also had crests usually erected.

The estate wherein we were privileged to have parked our Landrover and used as base made the owner and his staff almost self-sufficient. I suppose that country life in England in the eighteenth century was similar. Wheat was sown and harvested, flour ground and bread baked. Olive trees provided oil for cooking and lighting. All the vegetables and fruits were grown on the estate and the meat was always sheep and goats taken from the flocks. At the evening meal a charcoal fire was burning under

Storks.

the table and I learned that they produced their own charcoal. A long row of beehives provided honey and all their wine is pressed from the grapes in their vineyard. What surplus produce was sold and what necessities had to be bought I did not learn but I observed that the men were wearing sheepskin coats and the women thick woollen shawls. There was no telephone or radio and messages were exchanged by sending one of the men on a horse.

Within a few metres of our camp was an old olive tree, in a cleft of which there was the nest of a Tree Creeper; the parents were continuously going in and out to feed their nestling but we exposed no film on them because this species is very familiar to us at home. Only when we had all our gear packed and were ready to leave did Harvey take a close look through his binocular and realised that it was the Short-toed Treecreeper – *Carthia brachydactyla* – and therefore a new species for us and something rather special. Alas, it was too late to film it. A wonderful opportunity missed!

We watched a pair of Hawfinches which had a nest high up in an oak tree. Harvey climbed up to it and found it contained four eggs but it was too high to film easily and we do have it breeding occasionally at home. We did, however, enjoy good sightings of this largest of our finches with its bold colouring and enormous blue bill. Nearby was a bulky nest near the top of a cork oak and this proved to belong to a pair of Common Buzzards which were circling high overhead. There were two young buzzards nearly fledged and a large lizard partially eaten. A colony of Spanish Sparrows was established in the same tree; the cock birds look very like our House Sparrows at home though their habitat is less urban.

But the bird we had come so far to see, the Black-winged Kite, had thus far eluded us. All our local enquiries produced no information; whether this rare species had no interest for them or whether they wished to protect it and did not trust us, we could not decide. Even when we showed them a coloured illustration of the bird they merely shook their heads. Our search spread wider and wider from our base but it was not until we reached the upland pasture in the foothills of the mountains that we were rewarded. Here the shepherds watched their flocks on rolling hills that were not divided by any walls or fences. Spaced at wide intervals we could see each shepherd near his flock, often seated under a huge umbrella. We learned that they would live so for a week or more, cooking their simple food and sleeping under the umbrella.

Here we had our first sightings of the Black-winged Kite; it was a pair actually mating on the very top of one of the few trees in the area. It was doubtless their preoccupation that allowed us to approach them, though still half a kilometre away, and examine them through field glasses. Our first surprise was their small size; they were little more than half the size of the Red or Black Kite and the white tail was not deeply forked like that of other kites. Although usually described as white, its overall colour is rather a pale grey and the black is definitely on the shoulder and not on the whole wing. After the copulation they flew off on long pointed wings with a slow beat. We noticed that the wings are black underneath and the body and tail white. We searched diligently for a nest so that we might film this shy bird incubating or feeding young and eventually we found what we agreed must be it, but it was deserted. We kept watch for some days before examining it, but no parents came near. It was quite low down in an ilex oak and contained a single egg which was quite cold. The species is said to be crepuscular and might have been slipping in at dusk but the single cold egg convinced us that this nest had long since been deserted. The nest which was in a fork near the top of the tree, consisted of a platform of twigs with dead grass in the depression. The egg was coloured cream with brown markings. We were very disappointed.

We saw a cock Black-eared Wheatear making its display flight; this was the black-throated morph. Its appearance and habitat are very similar to our Wheatear at home but the back, nape and top of the head are coloured buff instead of grey. The hen was probably sitting on eggs in a hole in one of the many rocks in the area, but we failed to find it.

In the middle of the dirt road was an unfamiliar bird and we

Black-eared Wheatear

stopped the Landrover sufficiently far from it to avoid disturbing it as it appeared to be interested in some food source in the dirt. This was the Great Spotted Cuckoo and we had ample time to study and to film it. A handsome bird, larger than our Cuckoo, and having a white crest and a longer tail with white edges. The throat and breast are white; the back and wings dark brown flecked with white. We had time also to note the orange ring around the eyes. We were on our way to some high crags named Atalia near the castle of Marvao where we had been told the Eagle Owl nests. Indeed, my friends disturbed this huge bird roosting in a cleft of the cliff and filmed it briefly as it flew away until it was lost amongst the trees below the rocks. Sadly, I missed this splendid sight, having lost my way amongst the rocks and trees in returning to our parked vehicle.

We were seated on the shore of a reservoir near the River Nisa, arguing about the identity of some gulls on its surface, when we became interested in Swallows which were collecting mud from the side of a stream which flowed into the reservoir a few metres from us. Although at first sight we assumed this to be our familiar Barn Swallow, through glasses we realised at once that this was the much rarer Red-rumped Swallow which frequents southern Europe: its rump is a reddish-buff instead of blue and it lacks the bright red on the forehead and throat. Knowing of the very different nest this species builds, we followed their flight as they left repeatedly with a beakful of mud, and tracked them to a small stone bridge. Under this we found a small colony of their distinctive mud nests in process of building. They are shaped like flasks on their sides fastened to the underside of the bridge; the entrance is at the side through a narrow spout which opens up into the wider chamber where the eggs are incubated. I do not know the reason for this more elaborate structure unless it is a defence against snakes.

We had not ceased to enquire about the Great Bustard but it seemed we were in the wrong habitat for this magnificent bird which preferred the cultivated fields.

Meanwhile, we concentrated on filming the Little Bustards which were nesting in the upland pastures. A shepherd showed us

Little Bustard

how to locate a nest, for these birds are very wary, the nests were well hidden on the ground, and the approach of the hen to her nest was very circuitous and cautious.

While the hen is sitting on eggs, the cock keeps guard on higher ground a hundred metres or so distant. At the approach of any human or other predator he utters a strident alarm call and she crouches yet lower in her hidden nest. This was the signal to us that an incubating hen was in the vicinity and we had to judge from the terrain and ground cover where she might be. If we walked anywhere near the nest she would be off; but she would not fly directly from the nest; she would creep for twenty metres or so under cover and then take off. By noting where she broke cover and then following the furrow or ditch or dead ground, usually uphill, we would find the well-hidden nest. By this strategy we found several nests and put up hides at three of them, approaching the nest in several moves as this bird is very shy. It is a terrestrial inhabitant of southern Europe, about the size of a Pheasant but without the long tail. The hen is well camouflaged, being a sandy colour barred and streaked with brown, and paler beneath. The male is similar but with distinctive neck markings in black and white. The nest which I filmed contained four olive-green eggs, on which she sat in a very flattened posture. Long before I entered the hide she had left it but returned within twenty minutes and soon settled down. Initially she was uneasy at the whirring of the camera but soon came to ignore it completely. At the sound of a vehicle on the distant road she became very alert and often covered herself with loose vegetation; at the cock's grating alarm call she covered the eggs and crept away down the furrow and out of my sight.

We were much less successful in our attempts to record the Great Bustard on film. After much searching and questioning of local inhabitants brought no results, we sought the help of our host who offered to accompany us in our Landrover to a village several miles to the south where he knew a man who could show us where to look. This he did and we picked up a man who also entered the car and directed George where to drive up and down dirt roads dividing the fields of maize. When we had all despaired

Great-spotted Cuckoo

of finding our game, we turned a corner and suddenly came upon a huge cock Great Bustard, almost beneath the front wheels. I don't know whether we or the Bustard was the more surprised. We had expected a long and patient stalk, followed by the use of a telescopic lens and here the much-sought-after bird was at our feet. We tumbled out of the back of the Landrover just in time to see a huge body and thick neck and the white bristles below the chin when a tremendous spread of white wings with black tips lifted it up and over our vehicle to land a kilometre away. There it strutted with head erect, so we had a good view through binoculars and also shot a reel of film through my longest lens. The result was too distant but better than no record at all. We could note the long and powerful legs and the rich brown back flecked with black and the chestnut coloured band on the white breast. Our guide made us understand that it would run if we tried to approach nearer and that he had done very well to find one for us. Our host was anxious to return home so we decided to be content with our unusual close encounter.

It is good country for Nightingales and we often heard their lovely song at night but saw none in daylight. We found the nests of other warblers and had some difficulty in identifying those which were new to us. We decided that the nest in the ilex tree belonged to the Orphean Warbler because of the black cap and white outer tail feathers. The nest was low down and we filmed the parents from the Landrover and the parent birds were coming and going continuously. The cock was very similar in appearance to the Orphean but smaller and with a red ring round the eye. A third species had its nest about one metre above ground on top of a bramble bush; it contained four speckled eggs. We had good views of both parents which looked like so many other warblers – brown above and pale yellow below. This could have been the Icterine Warbler but we decided the legs were brown rather than black and we would not expect to find the Icterine in Portugal so it must be the Melodious Warbler. There were so many warblers and their songs were not so easy to pick out as they flitted about the fields and woodland but these were the only ones which are not found in England and which we could identify with some certainty.

There was a row of beehives near our camp site with a cloud of honey bees about it during all the hours of daylight. Hither came the Bee-eaters in their vivid livery of green and yellow, chestnut and black, swooping so fast and catching a bee in their long curved bill that we could not film them. We tried often to follow their flight as they returned with their prey to feed young which we knew would be waiting for them in nests at the end of a burrow in some earth bank or sandy cliff; but we always lost them. Nor could any local people tell us where is the colony of such nests. We thought that honey would make a pleasant addition to our diet and asked the owners to sell us some. They willingly produced a large jar of liquid honey taken out of the comb by a centrifuge and sealed with a cork, for which they would accept no money. We probably looked wretched and impoverished so with grateful thanks we took the jar to embellish our next meal. But when we had removed the cork we discovered scum on the top of the honey at least twenty-five millimetres thick which consisted of dead flies. This proved too much for me and I could not stomach the delicacy but my two companions were less fastidious.

In searching for the nest of the Red-legged Partridge, which we do not find in the North of England and desired to film, we disturbed a Nightjar from the edge of a wood. This was the Red-necked Nightjar, readily distinguished from our Nightjar at home by its white throat and red neck band. It shot up from the ground and we searched for the eggs or young which we knew must be there. We did this with the utmost care on our hands and knees because we knew how both are so wonderfully camouflaged that one could tread on them without seeing them. However, we found nothing. On two later occasions we looked in the same place and on each occasion one parent bird shot up from the ground, invisible to us until it moved, but we never found eggs or young. Of course, it makes no nest and pehaps it was roosting some distance from its progeny.

We put up a hide at the Red-legged Partridge's nest. It contained fourteen eggs, fawn background mottled with reddish-brown and somewhat larger than those of our Partridge. We saw mainly the hen which is more colourful than our game bird at home, having red legs, white throat and a black band dividing the throat from the brown mottled breast. But she would not return to the nest if one of us was in the hide, even at a considerable distance and we would not keep her from her eggs for more than ten minutes.

We saw many other interesting species – Rollers, Pratincoles, Crested Larks, and Blue Rock Thrush; but the time had come to leave. We took the same route home and saw a Booted Eagle on the road side and a Griffon Vulture circling high overhead as we crossed the mountain range with snow on the Sierre de Criedo but now we had a sudden urge to reach home.

We drove continuously through Spain and France by day and by night, taking turns at the wheel and stopping only to re-fuel. We had reserved a passage on the ferry from Le Havre on Monday morning, but it became obvious that we would arrive on Sunday evening and did not relish spending a night in our Landrover in the environs of Le Havre. Having therefore plenty of time and plenty of French francs left, we decided to indulge ourselves by having a night in an hotel to enjoy hot baths and a hot dinner. We stopped at a motel named Le Relais de Poitiers and were able to secure three rooms with bathrooms.

A hot bath was the greatest luxury as we had no opportunity to swim at our camp in Portugal. I wallowed in a deep bath for twenty minutes and when I emerged the bath looked like soup. So I emptied it, cleaned it thoroughly and had another. By the end of the second bath and with much scrubbing I felt clean. We had a wonderful dinner, a sweet night's sleep and an early breakfast. We arrived home in the early evening on Monday and on schedule. The English customs were very efficient and very polite. We had not had such treatment since we entered Portugal – our oldest ally.

CHAPTER TEN

The Isles of Paradise

The Seychelles are well so named for the archipelago lies like a scatter of ninety-two precious stones dropped in the Indian Ocean 5° south of the equator midway between Africa and India and 650 miles north of Madagascar.

Twenty-eight of these lovely islands are the tops of granite mountains rising from the ocean bed with some peaks nearly a thousand metres above sea level; others are flat coral reefs. The ocean surrounding them viewed from an inter-island aircraft looks sapphire or ultramarine, according to the depth. The largest and most populated island is Mahé, granitic and fringed with coral reefs, and divided by a rocky ridge running north and south with two peaks, the higher, Morne Seychellois, rising to nearly a thousand metres. Hither we went the easy way by jet aircraft, in part on holiday and in part to see and film the wonderful bird life.

This independent state became a popular holiday resort only in 1971 when tourists could travel by jet instead of by the long sea passage from Mombasa, since when tourism has become the main industry. The Seychelles have had a chequered career, annexed by the French in 1742, ceded to Britain in 1814, and declared independent in 1975. Since then local politics have played a major part in its fortunes. The language is a creole patois employing mostly French words with some English, Indian and Bantu words mingled in it. The people, cheerful and courteous, number about 60,000 on Mahé, 3,000 on Praslin and 1,000 on La Digue, with very few, if any, on the other islands. But throughout the history and the politics and the changing fortunes of the economy the smiling, sun-drenched islands remain a paradise on earth for tourists and botanists and ornithologists.

Of course, our first trip was to visit the 'Bird Island', a low sandy coral island clad with coconut palms, and the breeding

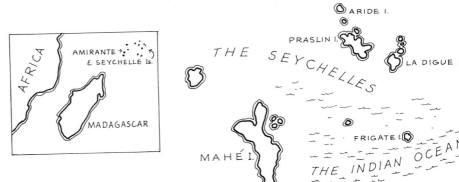

Sooty Terns

place of more than a quarter of a million Sooty Terns, which lay their two eggs in scrapes on the ground in June, hatch their young in August, and continue to feed them until October, by which time there are a million Sooty Terns on the ground and in the air, shouting for food, bringing fish and filling the air with their cries. The Sooty is not a particularly beautiful bird, but distinctive, being a deep black on top and white underneath, with a black bill, legs and feet. The black tail is deeply forked and there is a white patch on the forehead. It is a truly oceanic bird, being always at sea except during the breeding season.

To land on the island during the height of the nesting and feeding activity is a unique experience. The birds ignore the intruder; there are such huge numbers of them that the human presence is insignificant; we tread with extreme care to avoid standing on eggs or young; we cannot hear each other speak for the clamour; there is no attempt to mob us but we feel suffocated by the rush of wings. At one time the eggs and young were gathered by Seychellois and formed an important part of their diet, but they are now protected by law.

There are a few Bridled Terns and Noddies also on the island; these closely resemble the Sooty but are generally smaller and can be distinguished from them, the Bridled being grey on top and the Noddy being a rather dull brown all over and having a rounded end to its tail. Elsewhere among the islands we saw Caspian, Crested, Little and Saunder's Terns. As might be expected, it is an ideal area for sea birds.

Among the many passerines flitting about the palm trees, I noticed the familiar Spotted Flycatcher which we know so well at home. I was told that it had not then been recorded as a migrant or even as an accidental in the Seychelles so I was at pains to film it though with more difficulty than success.

As I walked around the small island on the sandy shore close to the rippling waves at my feet I was disturbed by a violent rush of water coming towards me. This was made by a fish being pursued by a small shark; it came through the shallows at such speed that it shot out of the water and landed on the sand at my feet. The shark realised its peril just in time and managed somehow to go into

Seychelles Kestrel

reverse; its back was clear out of the water by the time it was able to stop and flounder back into deeper water. It was small as sharks go, about two metres long. Before I could decide whether to throw the fish back into the sea, where doubtless the shark would take it, a Seychellois boy picked it up, knocked it on the head with a stone, and made off with it.

But the Fairy Tern is in my opinion the most attractive of all the terns. We found it on the island named Cousin which we reached by boat from the Bird Island. There was a European girl living there who acted as warden and guide; she received the boat load of tourists who waded ashore onto a sandy beach. She wanted to organise us all into a 'Sunday School' party to accompany her on a circuitous tour of the island but one or two of us decided that we would prefer to remain stationary to see what wildlife came within our vision. She took this rather badly as a slight on her guiding ability and, because I had a 700 mm lens on my movie camera, decided I must be a professional photographer and therefore needed a licence to take photographs. She took some persuading otherwise.

I was pleased to have stayed because I was able to watch the Fairy Terns among the casuarina trees. This is one of the smaller terns and all white except for a black upturned bill, black legs and unwebbed feet and a black ring around the eye. Its peculiarity is that it lays a single egg on top of a tree branch and glues it thereon before brooding it in that precarious position. It may breed in any month and when the spotted blue egg or a fledgling does fall, it is snapped up by a lizard. I was told that less than a quarter of the eggs laid result in an adult bird: one might suppose this species to be in danger of extinction, but there are estimated to be ten thousand pairs breeding on the island of Cousin so it must fare better than I supposed. There were many small doves rustling among the fallen palm fronds; these proved to be the Little Barred Ground Dove which is not indigenous but has been imported from Australia. Several of the common birds on these islands have been introduced from abroad, such as the Mynah from India, which is omnivorous and friendly.

There are, however, many interesting birds to be found, some of them being endemic. One of these is the Black Parrot and I particularly wanted to film this. I found a Seychellois boy who was interested in birds and willing to guide a small party of tourists through the forest in the Vallée de Mai on Praslin where it might be found. He and I outstripped the others, I carrying my camera with a long lens and tripod and he occasionally making an imitative call. Presently the Black Parrot answered and they continued to call back and forth until he whispered to me that the bird was in sight. With my binocular I could just discern it high in a palm tree and almost hidden by the thick foliage. In great excitement I put the camera on the tripod and focused onto the parrot. He went back down the trail to the following party to stop them until I had shot my film. Unfortunately his limited command of English and his own excitement misled them; they thought he was urging them to catch up with me to see this rare sight. Just as I had the bird clearly in my camera sights with exposure and focus correctly set and my finger on the button to start it rolling, up they came at speed, chattering loudly among themselves and off flew the parrot, never to be seen by us again. The looks which I and the guide gave them were blacker than the parrot. In fact, this parrot is not really black; it is dark grey or brown with black legs and a grey beak but it is unmistakable, being shaped like a parrot but lacking the usual bright colours of that genus. It is unique to the island of Praslin, which is strange for so strong a flyer, and it is rarely seen outside the Vallée de Mai. There also is found the unique tree, coco de mer, which produces the strange double coconut that was for so many years a complete mystery to naturalists when washed up on foreign shores. Whether there is any connection between the Black Parrot and the unique coco de mer, both confined to Praslin, I do not know. The bird was for many years persecuted because of its depredation of fruit trees, but is now wholly protected. Hopefully its numbers may now increase from the present twenty to thirty birds.

Another rarity is the Seychelles Kestrel which has been honoured by specific distinction, being the smallest of the several species of kestrel. A student was making a detailed study of the

Seychelles Kestrel whilst we were there and had located seven nests of pairs on Mahé which has most of the population. He let me examine one immature he had taken from the nest as a fledgling but I could see little difference between it and the Lesser Kestrel except that it is perhaps smaller, the chestnut back is more heavily marked with black and the cream-coloured breast less so; the crown and tail of both have a blue tinge and both have the pointed wings of the true falcon. There are probably fewer than a hundred pairs of this species in the Seychelles and the numbers are diminishing due to introduced cats, rats and Barn Owls, which latter compete with them for nesting sites. Despite Government protection this dainty little falcon suffers from man's predation, being considered by the ignorant to be unlucky as a resident in the roof of one's house and also because of its reputation for taking young chickens. The Kestrels of Madagascar, Mauritius, Aldabra and the Seychelles have all been given separate specific status but may all have developed separately on their islands from original South African stock. I was pleased to have this opportunity to examine the young Seychelles Kestrel, which was in good health and seemed to be quite content in captivity on its perch, and which was soon to be released into the wild. I hope the result of the survey will be even better protection for this rare species.

Another rarity, which I was privileged to see in different circumstances; is the Seychelles Bare-legged Scops Owl. During the first half of this century it was thought to be extinct but in the latter half there have been a few sightings by reliable observers and its distinctive call at night has been more often heard in the mountain forests than the bird has been seen. It is believed to nest in rocky clefts in the mountains but the man I knew had found a nest high in a tree on the mountainous ridge above Victoria on Mahé. He would not lead John and me to the nest but he promised us a sight of the male bird if we would accompany him on a night expedition. This we gladly did and we stopped on the road in the vicinity of the nest. I am against the attraction of birds by playing back taped recordings of their various calls but I overcame my objection for the sake of seeing this rare bird. Our guide had taped the call of the male which sounded like a two-man saw and this recording was almost immediately answered by a similar call about a mile away. He continued to play it for a few seconds at intervals of three minutes and each time it was answered by a similar call progressively nearer at hand. Obviously the male parent hunting at a distance from the nest was disturbed by the apparent presence of another male close to its nest.

On the fifth response which came from a tree only some ten metres from our car, the guide switched on a spotlight and focused the beam on this small brown owl, about half the size of a Barn Owl and much darker, with large yellow eyes, fully in view. It would have small ear-tufts and legs quite bare of any feathers but I cannot be sure of having seen these or just imagined them in the few seconds in which the bird was clearly visible. I took a still photograph with flash which did not come out too well.

Another rarity is the Brush Warbler which I was lucky to see on Cousin and which is only found on this tiny island. It is strongly territorial and this may account for the very small numbers surviving. It has a melodious song like most warblers but differs from others in this family by laying usually a single egg. The French name for the species likens it to a small Blackbird and this is perhaps due to its song being not unlike that of our European Blackbird. A common bird in all the islands is the Madagascar Fody, usually named the Cardinal because of the bright red colour of the male. It is a small finch with a high-pitched note, which has been introduced by man into the islands from Madagascar and has established itself very well. The female is coloured rather a dull brown, but the male bird demands to be photographed.

In the harbour at Victoria, when the tide was out, there was always a good collection of waders feeding on the mudflats, mostly migrants in their winter dress – Whimbrels, Turnstones, Sanderlings, Little Stints, Grey or Black-bellied Plovers, and Curlew Sandpipers. But the one I particularly wanted to film was the Crab Plover and there were plenty of them. There was no time left to visit La Digue to look for the Black Paradise

Bare-legged Scops Owl

Flycatcher or the island of Frigate to find the Magpie Robin: these must await another visit to these glorious islands. Hopefully Government protection will safeguard these rare species against the mounting pressure of tourists and the avid predation of collectors.

Mynah

CHAPTER ELEVEN

The Isles of the Wanderers

The Farne Islands lie just a few miles off the coast of Northumberland, and very accessible to George and myself who have landed on them many times as day tourists. They are not the tops of ancient volcanoes or built up from the ocean bed by coral insects like most of the islands we have visited, but are the last outcrop of the Great Whin Sill, over which on the mainland tumble spectacular waterfalls. They present sheer cliffs to the onslaught of the North Sea waves and provide excellent nesting sites for several species of sea birds.

Their name derives from the Anglo-Saxon words *Farena Ealandr* which mean 'the Isles of the Wanderers' because they were inhabited at one time by a tribe which used them as a winter base, whilst in summer it roamed on the mainland as nomads. It is said that they prayed for stormy weather because only then could they be sure they would not be attacked by Vikings. Now the only wanderers are the sea birds which travel thousands of miles to breed on these islands relatively secure from predators and with ready access to the cold waters of the North Sea to provide food. The islands are also a staging post for thousands of migrant birds in spring and autumn passage which breed in the high north.

In the seventh century St Cuthbert built his hermit's cell on the island nearest to the coast, Inner Farne, and for nine hundred years monks used to row across from the sand dunes when the sea was not too rough. Thus there is a great Christian tradition associated with these islands and also with the adjacent Holy Island or Lindisfarne, which is inhabited and boasts a fine Castle and a pub, but not so many birds.

The Farne Islands now belong to the National Trust which safeguards this heritage, controls the flow of visitors, and provides wardens to protect the birds during the breeding season. St Cuthbert was the first conservationist for he blessed the Eider

Ducks and decreed they must never be molested, for which act this species is known locally as St Cuthbert's Duck. But after the monks left and until the National Trust provided protection, the collection of eggs was a local industry.

Landing is now allowed on only two of the islands and permits are needed for which a small charge is made. Boats are hired in Seahouses from licensed boat owners and their numbers are strictly limited. Even so, there is great disturbance to the nesting terns as visitors come ashore.

The National Trust acquired the islands in 1925 and recorded the objectives of their management as preserving the natural aspect and features of the islands, the birds and other animal life thereon and the buildings and other man-made structures and providing for and controlling public access so as not to conflict therewith.

George and I were invited to make a film of the wildlife on the islands and were given permission to land on any of them and to stay overnight when necessary. We were thus able to do most of our filming in the early morning before the tourists arrived and later when they had left. We decided to make monthly visits of a few days each in April to July so as to record the arrival of the breeding birds, the pairing, and selection of nest sites, the laying and incubation of eggs, the rearing of young, and finally their departure. We would record as many different species as we could, moving from one island to another with help from the wardens who maintain radio contact with the shore.

On arrival at Seahouses on a Friday afternoon we garaged the car and carried our equipment down to the harbour where we expected to find the coble we had booked for the passage ready for our embarkation. We were disappointed to be told that the sea was too rough to enable a landing. We looked seaward from the end of the pier and had to agree that the waves seemed formidable and a north-east gale was blowing. The skipper hoped it might abate in the evening and said we should wait. We did. We waited for hours, periodically finding the skipper to enquire about the prospects. He is taciturn always but on this occasion filled with utmost gloom. We almost despaired but held on,

Bamburgh Castle

leaned over the sea-wall and wished the wind to drop.

It was already dark when his crew approached us. Without any preliminaries he said in his delightful Northumbrian accent 'Where's your gear?' and we joyfully collected our gear – rucksacks, cameras and hides. It was a hazardous passage and a rough landing but we did eventually reach Inner Farne and made our way to the ancient hermitage, which has been restored sufficiently for the wardens to live there during the summer months.

On this first visit in April the breeding season had scarcely begun. Shags have been feeding around the island and up and down the coast all winter; as early as January they have looked for nest sites and even started some desultory nest building but they do not lay eggs until March. Now they are incubating four green eggs and occasionally turning them over as they sit on their solid nests built of sea-weed. They nest colonially but never so close together that adjacent birds could reach one another with outstretched necks. Both parents share the task of incubation and the returning male often brings a piece of sea-weed as an offering to the female, which adds it to the nest before the change-over.

This is one of the oldest species of living birds, having been here on earth millions of years before man made his appearance. The unfledged young soon after hatching have a very reptilian appearance. But adults in their breeding plumage look very handsome with a green gloss on their black plumage and a stiff upright crest. There is a cloud of Kittiwake flying about the rocky ledges and the Shags hiss at them if they fly too low over them, exposing a bright yellow gape. The Kittiwakes are contesting for the most desirable nesting sites where they may build their strong nests and the air is filled with the clamour of their cries. Some of the disputes end in fights but most of the apparent fights are actually displays to prospective mates.

Guillemots are standing in hundreds on top of the Pinnacle rocks on Staple Island. As they are all facing outwards, we know that they have not yet started to lay their single egg on the bare rock.

Most of the Puffins are still swimming in huge rafts on the

Guillemot

Puffin

heaving sea but a few of the early arrivals have landed on grassy mounds and are busily clearing out the burrows in the soil which they used last year. They have already acquired the brilliantly coloured outer shell on their strange parrot-shaped bills.

We see a Purple Sandpiper resting on its passage to the north where its breeding habitat may be in Arctic Norway. There are Oystercatchers calling their shrill piping cry, having just returned to their chosen breeding area; and Ringed Plovers are busily running about on prospective nesting sites.

Now the Eider drakes may be seen on shore or swimming in the shallows near it. They are strikingly handsome birds, heavily built and with a curious wedge-shaped head, white with a black crown and a green patch on the nape. The upper parts are white with a pink tinge on the breast; the belly is black. The duck is a mottled brown all over to provide excellent camouflage when she is sitting on her nest on the ground. She sits very close on four to six pale green eggs in a capacious nest lined with feathers plucked from her own breast – the famous eiderdown; but if she is disturbed, she will cover the eggs with the down before leaving and will not move far away. This is a diving duck, which is seldom seen on land except during the breeding season. They nest regularly in big numbers on most of the islands of the Farnes but are not so cherished as in Iceland where the nests are stripped of their down when the young leave. The other two species of Eider Duck, the King Eider and Steller's Eider breed further north.

As soon as the ducks have laid their clutch of eggs the males leave them and go back to the sea where they sometimes may be seen flying in single file low over the water. Their call is a distinctive croon ending in a grunt.

On our next visit towards the end of May, we landed on Longstone, the home of Grace Darling who in 1838 with her father saved the lives of eight passengers and crew from the wrecked *Forfarshire*, which aroused the admiration of the Victorian public. They raised a subscription for her so that she might live in comfort on shore but, alas, she died at an early age of tuberculosis.

We went to Longstone to film the colony of grey seals which

Eider Drakes

haul out on the flat rocks on the eastern shore. The calves are born in October and November on the more remote islands and were fully grown and mingled with the cows; there was one bull in the herd and two others on Hopper Rock. The bull at Longstone End had a tremendous gash in the chest which we assumed had resulted from fighting another bull. Their coats are mainly grey but are streaked and spotted with black and white in a great variety of patterns. Whilst being so graceful in the water, they are ungainly on land and move across the rocks with great heavings of their clumsy bodies. There are said to be between 900 and 1,000 breeding females in the colony and, a much smaller number of bulls, but the population is not stable. We counted about forty hauled out on our visit but we did not stay too long as they appeared to become agitated and some started to heave their way towards the sea.

We were landed on Inner Farne and met the four wardens living on it who showed us where to stow our gear. The Chief Warden was appropriately named Mr Wren.

What a change has taken place in the six weeks since our previous visit. Now the cliffs and rocks are crowded with sea birds; the air is filled with terns flying and hovering and crying with a great clamour; and there are great rafts of Puffins bobbing up and down offshore before flying inland with whirring wings to choose their nesting burrow.

Four species of tern breed on the Farnes and upward of seven thousand of them have arrived between mid-April and the end of May. The Arctic Tern comes in the greatest number – about two and a half thousand pairs – and this beautiful pelagic bird is indeed a wanderer for it travels thousands of miles in its migration and never appears to rest on the water.

As one hovers above his nest among the sea campion, we have a perfect view at close range of its elegant white body and tail, grey wings, and sharply contrasting black crown. But the most striking features are the blood-red bill and the almost transparent white tail fanned out as it hovers. Its defiant scream bids us move back as she lowers herself onto the scrape, which is all her nest. We do so quickly for she is quite capable of pecking a scalp and

Arctic Terns

drawing blood. We set up two hides among the hundreds of nests on the ground and leave them empty for the birds to become accustomed to them.

We rose at 05.00 next morning, cooked a hasty breakfast, and were ensconced in our hides to start filming as soon as the light was sufficient. George concentrated on the Arctic Tern and I on the Common Tern. This latter is almost indistinguishable from the Arctic in winter but now it is easy to tell them apart; the bill of the Common is an orange-red with a black tip; it is also slightly smaller and the tail streamers a little shorter. The two species do not segregate their nests so we had the advantage of comparing the two species at close range. The usual clutch of eggs is two and occasionally three, very ovoid, and beautifully marked, black on brown; the eggs of the two species show no difference. The hens fussed a lot whilst incubating, shuffling on their eggs and putting finishing touches to their rudimentary nests. Once there was a 'dread', which we both filmed. For no apparent reason all the sitting terns rose together into the air screaming tumultuously. The air was filled with wheeling birds in sudden panic; and then, as if controlled by a single mind, they flew out to sea in a white cloud and soon returned to settle quietly on their nests. I have never heard any adequate explanation of this phenomenon and we were fortunate to see and film it.

After three hours we moved one hide to a nearby area where the Sandwich Terns had congregated their nests to film them next day. Then we filmed Shags and Kittiwakes from the cliff top, looking down on their nests, the former having two naked and ugly black-skinned young in them, and the latter two brown mottled eggs. We found many Eider nests where the ducks sat tight but in one it seemed that the eggs were near to hatching so I determined to film them at first light in the morning. I knew the ducklings would leave the nest immediately they hatched and this was an opportunity that might not recur. Then the first boat-load of visitors arrived so we filmed people instead of birds and they were almost as interesting.

The tide was low which necessitated landing over a plank from boat to shore instead of onto the jetty. This caused much hilarity.

The terns' nests were protected by confining the visitors with ropes and posts to a path from shore to the lighthouse. The whole colony of terns rose from their nests in a clamour as the visitors walked up the path. Many terns made courageous attacks at the heads of the intruders, most of whom took it in the right spirit. I did, however, hear one man say to his girl friend that all these birds should be shot. Notices remind the visitors that this is a nature reserve and generally they appear to obey the rules but there is no doubt that each boat-load causes a great disturbance. As sitting birds leave their nests in haste, eggs may be damaged or rolled out of the nest and thieving Herring Gulls are always ready to steal unprotected eggs. Some small boys cannot resist the temptation to do the same in spite of the watchful wardens.

In the afternoon we were taken to Brownsman Island where another two wardens were living in an old tower, formerly a beacon lighthouse; it was partially destroyed by storm some two hundred years ago but has now been repaired to provide accommodation for the wardens. Here we were made welcome by Bob Gomes. They ferried us across to Staple Island to film the Guillemots crowded on the tops of the towering columns of rock named the Pinnacles.

This is indeed a wonderful sight. About a thousand pairs of the southern race of the Guillemot raise their single chicks on the densely packed summit and precarious ledges of these columns rising sheer from the sea. The females are sitting each on its egg on the bare rock and in close proximity; the males are standing nearby or coming and going with food. How they find space to land, much less to locate their mate, is a wonder. Those standing or sitting now all face inwards. The eggs are very varied in background colour – blue, mottled with brown and black; and they are strongly ovoid in shape so that, when they are moved, they do not roll off a ledge. The congestion is caused by the popularity of these sites which provide freedom from all predators except the Herring Gull and the Lesser Black-backed Gull, which would carry off eggs or chicks left unprotected. However, the Guillemots are good parents and one or other is always on guard.

The boatmen at Seahouses pronounce the name as if it were spelled 'willymoo' and, of course, they are right because our word comes from the French name for William – *Guillaume*. The Manx name is *Gwilym*. It is just another example of a common and likeable bird being given a Christian name. It is sometimes called the foolish Guillemot for the obvious reason that it stands around helplessly while men take the eggs; but it has other local names – Willock, Marrock, Scuttock, and Murreseahen.

We noticed that a few of these birds have a white eye-ring and a white line running from it on each side of the head to the nape. This morph is known as the Bridled Guillemot but it is not a separate species. The proportion of bridled birds to the remainder of the colony in the Farnes is only about four per cent but this increases in more northern colonies up to about fifty percent in Spitzbergen. I wondered if this marking is genetically connected with the ability to withstand colder climate. A few single Black Guillemots may be seen in most years around the Farnes but they never breed here. It is a smaller bird with all black plumage except for white wing patches. Its feet are a vivid scarlet instead of black.

Another species of the Auk family which breeds every year in the Farnes is the Razorbill but the number of breeding pairs is less than one percent of the Guillemots. These are also black and white sea birds but the bill is compressed laterally and has an obvious white line marked vertically on it. It stands upright like the Guillemot and associates freely with it, nesting on the same ledges. Both are very noisy birds in the breeding territory and there is a constant sound of growls and grunts with an occasional whistle from the Razorbills.

The much smaller Little Auk never breeds here but large numbers do pass through the islands on their autumn passage.

On returning to Brownsman we went to the colony of Cormorants nesting at one end of it in the centre of the island. The bulky nests are of seaweed and the parents sit very close because if the eggs are left exposed for a moment, the Black-backed Gulls and Herring Gulls are ready to steal and eat them.

We had no problem to film the Cormorants on the nest without disturbing them. They are larger than the Shag but very similar; the black plumage has a bronze sheen in place of the green tinge of the Shag, and it has no crest. It is not exclusively maritime but will follow up rivers and is seen sometimes on freshwater lakes. It has white patches on the cheeks and white patches on the thighs during the breeding season. The day is warm and the sitting birds have a very noticeable gular flutter, which is one means of dissipating excess heat. Another means of thermal control when these birds are standing on rocks is to spread their wings – 'hanging out their wings to dry'. Some people think their feathers are less waterproofed than those of other diving and underwater-swimming birds and need to be dried between dives; but they may often be seen preening and re-oiling their feathers so I think thermal control is more likely.

We went back to Inner Farne to spend the night so that we might film the young Eider ducklings leaving the nest. I was in position in the hide at first light and it was obvious that some of the eggs had already hatched. After half an hour's wait there was some movement by the duck; she came off the nest and I could see that there were ten ducklings, and all eggs hatched. The precocial little ones immediately started to leave the nest and to follow her in single file, struggling valiantly to clamber over tufts of grass. Sometimes an unmated duck will come along to help the mother as a self-appointed 'universal aunt' but with this brood it was unnecessary; she could cope with that number though they did straggle a bit before they reached the rain pool to which she was leading them. Later in the day we saw they had reached the sea and were swimming in line behind their mother towards the mainland shore two miles away, where the feeding is better suited to their needs. Bobbing like corks on the surface of the waves they managed to swim closely after the parent but we noticed that the brood had been reduced to eight. There are so many predators waiting to seize these helpless little creatures on this first hazardous journey that the clutch size may be halved by the time they reach safety. But the original number of eggs evidently allows for this and there is no danger of this fine species becoming extinct in the Farnes.

Kittiwakes

Eider Duck

We returned to sleep the night on Brownsman and breakfasted with the wardens at 06.00. In daylight we saw nests of Arctic Terns very close to the building and so numerous and congested it was difficult to avoid stepping on them. Eider Ducks also had nests everywhere and we could film both species from a bench outside the doorway without hides. The male terns were bringing in sand eels; we watched one being mobbed by three hens as soon as he landed. One of them seized the loose end of a sand eel hanging from his bill but he decided that she was not his mate and refused to release it. The tug-of-war continued for five minutes when the female finally won the prize and this disconsolate male flew off to find another meal for his true mate, who had been standing patiently throughout the struggle.

We found two nests of Oystercatchers, each with two eggs and also one of a Ringed Plover with three eggs; we put up hides at each to move closer on the following day, and later we filmed them coming onto their eggs. Both species are shy and approach their nests very warily. The long red bill of the Oystercatcher is conspicuous and the parents will not go near the nest, which is just a scrape on the ground, if they think they are observed. Once on the nest, however, they keep the head and bill low to the ground. Male and female take turns at incubation and the change-over is performed with great caution.

We accompanied the wardens in their rubber dinghy onto Staple to film them controlling the population of Herring Gulls and Lesser Black-backed Gulls nesting among the sea campion on the flat top of the island. These two species multiply so fast and are so predatory on the eggs and young of other species that some control of their numbers is essential if other species are to survive on the Farnes. The wardens do this by injecting formalin into the air sac of newly laid eggs which prohibits development into a chick. If they were to remove the eggs, the hen would merely lay again; and if they were to use any other method of sterilisation, the egg would lose weight and the parent would push it out of the nest and lay another to replace it. They painted a yellow band round each egg sterilised so that they would know on their next visit that it had been treated. Thereafter the gulls would sit happily on the sterile eggs until the breeding season had ended.

The nests of both species are similar and we could not distinguish between them; both are bulky and numerous and apparently intermingled amongst the vegetation.

The preservation of the vegetation on this and other islands is a matter of concern to the National Trust. There are rabbits on Brownsman of an unusual ginger colour, descendants of a pair brought from the mainland by fishermen. These and the Puffins decimate the vegetation and erode the soil with their burrows. On other islands, where the grey seals breed, the soil covering is also threatened.

The wardens had erected a series of wood and wire-netting boxes, one inside another, with different meshes of netting, to establish which animal was causing most damage to the vegetation.

Wardens took us in the dinghy to another island, North Wamses, to take a series of shots of the Cormorants which nest there. Lesser Black-backed and Herring Gulls were also nesting and some of their eggs had been sterilised. Puffins were going in and out of their burrows.

It was not until our visit in mid-June that we spent time on that most attractive species of the Auk family, the Puffin. It is estimated that some twenty thousand pairs breed each year on the Farne Islands and they come early in April and leave about the end of July to spend the rest of the year at sea around the coasts of Europe. They nest colonially on the islands which have a good covering of earth and vegetation, nesting in the burrows of rabbits or in ones they excavate themselves. The ground may be so riddled with burrows that it caves in as one walks over it. When an area has been too much undermined, they move elsewhere, leaving a dereliction behind.

The scientific name of the Shearwater genus is Puffinus and the type species of that genus is the Manx Shearwater, *Puffinus puffinus*, whereas the scientific name of the Puffin is *Fratercula arctica*. This is indeed confusing and it arises from an error when a young Manx Shearwater was taken from a burrow in the Isle of Man under the mistaken belief that it was a Puffin that was sent to

London for identification.

The attractive little Puffin is essentially a comical bird. It is black on top and white underneath with white cheeks and orange coloured feet; its special feature is the triangular bill, shaped somewhat like that of a parrot, laterally flattened, and striped red, yellow and blue. This gaudy appendage alters in winter to a smaller size and is no longer brightly coloured. It is this harlequin appearance and its upright stance on the cliff tops, its waddling gait and its rapidly whirring wings as it comes in to land that provide the sense of comedy. But the parents take life very seriously and are assiduous in providing food for their single chick lying safely in its burrow. It is said that one bird may fly thirty miles on a single fishing trip and may be away for one and a quarter hours.

We watched them take off from the cliff edge to descend with whirring wings to the sea far below and returning with their small wings widespread and feet thrust far apart to achieve a safe landing. These short wings make very efficient paddles under water when the stubby streamlined body is pursuing a fish. We saw them landing with as many as seven sand eels, held in the bill and I used to wonder how the bird under water could possibly hold two or three and yet catch more. By careful observation I decided that they are held under the tongue within the beak, the ends hanging out at each side. The food is thrust into the beak of the young chick one by one in the early stages of its development and each parent stays below ground for several minutes; but later the whole catch is dropped on the floor of the burrow and the chick is left to feed itself as the parents hurtle out to find more food.

At this stage the chick is a bundle of soft grey feathers and grows as large as the parents before it first emerges to the mouth of the burrow to survey the wonderful world of pink flowering sea campion and the blue sea far below. At the least alarm it retreats into the safety of its dark home.

On Staple Island there is a deep gully, known as Kittiwake Gully, which is a favourite nesting place for these beautiful gulls. Because it is so narrow and so deep with numerous ledges on

Herring Gull

either side, it is an ideal place for observing this species incubating eggs and feeding young; the parents are so accustomed to visitors and so secure from too close an approach that we had no need for a hide to film them. They are magnificent aerial performers, hanging on the up-currents of air with motionless wings or landing delicately at the nest on a narrow ledge. As we watched, one of the wardens leaned over the edge to collect two chicks for the purpose of ringing them. This he did very expertly and causing the young birds no apparent stress nor the parents any prolonged alarm, although they made plenty of noise while he did it.

This lovely gull is familiar round all our shores during the breeding season but spends the rest of the year far out at sea. where it often follows ships. It is a glistening white except for the black wing tips and its bill is yellow; the dark eyes have a red ring around them. The chicks, however, are a silvery grey with soft juvenile feathers.

We encountered a small party of Shelduck young being led from their nest to the shore. They were larger than the Eider ducklings we had filmed earlier and more prettily marked with brown stripes on yellow. They dropped one by one into a rocky pool, the parent keeping well out of our sight. The drake is a large and handsome bird, black and white with a chestnut band across his chest and some green about the head. A few pairs breed each year on the Farnes but they breed generally inland and may be seen during the remainder of the year close in-shore and in estuaries.

We watched a bird which is more common than it used to be, not only on the Farnes, but all around our shores, the Fulmar. This large gull-like sea bird is a petrel, having the tubular nostrils on top of the bill typical of their genus; it is more heavily built than other petrels but spends like them most of the year at sea, gliding close above the waves and in the troughs. It nests singly on most of the islands and on the adjacent shore where it lays its single egg in a grassy nest on a ledge. If approached on the nest it has an unpleasant habit of ejecting a squirt of evil-smelling oil at the intruder. I have suffered this attack and it takes some time to

Shelducklings

remove the smell.

We both spent several hours in the hide filming the large colony of some 300 pairs of Sandwich Terns nesting on Inner Farne. This large tern has a forked tail without streamers; it is white below and grey above, with a black crown and nape and black legs. Two distinctive features are the bill, which is black with a yellow tip, and black feathers projecting from the rear of the crown. By the end of the breeding season the black crown is receding and the black crest is streaked with white, giving it the appearance of a worried parent. Indeed, this seemed to us accountable to the problem of keeping the rapidly growing chicks satisfied with food. The nests were very close together and the precocial chicks roamed throughout the colony as soon as hatched. Hundreds of adult birds were coming and going all the time. Whenever one landed with food there was a rush to it of chicks and we could discern the concern of the parent to decide which were its own and to avoid feeding a neighbour's. All the chicks looked alike to us and it was a mystery how parents eventually identified their own, which they often did not do at the first attempt.

Puffins

The fourth species of tern, the Roseate Tern, does not breed on the Farnes every year and, when it does, the number of breeding pairs is small. We were fortunate in that there were ten pairs breeding on Brownsman that year and we had the chance to film this comparatively rare visitor incubating eggs at the end of June. This vividly white tern also has a black crown but its bill is black with a little red at the base. On arrival there is a pink tinge on the breast, hence its specific name, but it soon loses this. We took the greatest care not to disturb these females on the nest and filmed from a long distance.

We came back again to the islands in the last week of July to find a vastly different scene. There were a few young Kittiwakes on the cliff ledges being fed by their parents but most had flown. The young Shags and Cormorants were all on the water. The odd-looking gulls still hanging around on land were juveniles of the Herring Gull and Lesser Black-backed Gull which were indistinguishable, being mottled brown all over with black bills, and bearing no resemblance to their parents. They were being fed

occasionally but must soon launch out to sea to feed themselves.

Nearly all the Puffins had left; a few burrows still showed a fully grown and well fledged chick at the mouth, waiting to be fed. Probably the first breeding attempt had failed. Eider Ducks and their young had all left the islands but considerable numbers were swimming offshore. We saw an Arctic Skua, the dark morph, with its typical tail and dashing flight, engaged on its piratical errand of pursuing any gull with a fish until it disgorged it.

We re-visited some of the Fulmar nests and found the single chicks had grown to an enormous size. Pale grey in colour, they regarded us without alarm but showed no tendency to move out of the nest. The adult birds, which do not look colourful in the air, have beautiful plumage when seen at close quarters, especially around the stubby neck. These are the lighter morph with the head, breast and belly white and black wings and grey tail. Their voice is a hoarse grunt. They leave the single chick, bloated with regurgitated oil and so fat it can scarcely move, until the excess fat is used up and hunger compels it to make a move. Then on too weak legs it shuffles to the edge of the ledge and drops off to glide down to the sea. There it may float for two or three days before hunger drives it to learn how to fish.

Gannets, those expert fishers, which breed further north, were far out to sea, plunging from a height directly into the sea. The crowded tops of the Pinnacles were empty of Guillemots and Razorbills and only a few of these species could be observed out at sea. The terns had all deserted their teeming nurseries and most had left for warmer climates. Only the gulls were plentiful, staying with us all the year round.

Another breeding season at the Farnes had ended. The raucous tumult had died away and the cries of gulls and fulmars were muted by the sound of breaking waves on the rocks. Soon the migrants would arrive to stay for a few hours or days to feed and rest on their annual journeys to the south. The ebb and flow of birds is like the ebb and flow of the tides which wash perpetually these northern rocks.

We had planned to leave Brownsman on Monday but the tourist boat, the *Glad Tidings*, never came. There was a strong wind blowing and the waves were white-capped but we never suspected she would not put out. Towards evening the warden sent a radio message to the shore and learned that the sea was too rough to take us off; there is no jetty on Brownsman and embarkation from the rocks necessitates calm weather. The sailors are rightly fearful for their boats. We went to sleep on the floor after a short prayer for clement weather, unlike the earlier inhabitants of these islands who prayed for storms. The weather next day was decidedly worse – high wind from the east, rain like stair rods and the waves beating on rocks and flinging spray upwards as if reaching for the Pinnacles. We radioed the shore to pass on a message to our wives who we envisaged would by now be organising a memorial service.

The irony of our situation was lamentable. By ordinary circumstances we would have welcomed an extra day on these lovely islands but we could not photograph in such weather and few birds were flying. We watched the Fulmars exhibit their grace and skill in combating the fierce gusts and landing adroitly on a ledge. We watched the Gannets plunging and the 'white horses' breaking and the flung spray – and we waited. I always thought I could watch moving water endlessly without boredom, whether it be a fast-flowing stream, or waves or a waterfall, but my mind had tossed enough upon the ocean and I wanted home. We had brought food for three days and there was enough to spare for the fourth but the prospect for the remainder of the week looked grim. The wardens offered to share their rations with us but we were reluctant to diminish them.

That evening Peter Hawkey radioed us that the wind was abating and he hoped to pick us up on Wednesday if the weather continued to improve. About midday we heard the diesel engine of his small motorboat, bade the wardens farewell, and managed to embark our cameras and gear without being soaked. There were still big rollers to be negotiated by Peter's small craft, which he managed most skilfully, creeping from the lee of one island to another and then close inshore to Seahouses harbour. We were glad to be ashore and most grateful to him for relieving our maroon.

CHAPTER TWELVE

The Last Frontier

The lion's roar sounded to me unpleasantly close. My companion, Reiner, said it was at least half a mile away and gave no cause for concern; it was merely summoning the pride to organise the evening hunt.

I was lying on my back in my sleeping-bag on the ground between his pick-up truck and a blazing fire and was staring up at the unfamiliar constellations which glittered so much more brightly than at home. A Nightjar was circling beneath the branches of a nearby tree but I could not see it well enough to ascertain which of the several species of South African Nightjars it might be; they differ by the number of white spots on their wonderfully camouflaged brown plumage.

'Cover your face with your sleeping-bag before you go to sleep,' said Reiner. 'A hyena would bite off your face if it is left exposed and one came by. There are plenty of them around.' I covered my head and shut out the stars, not relishing the idea of becoming one of the faceless ones.

Reiner and I were driving through Kavango to enter the Caprivi Strip and to follow the Okavango river to the border of Botswana where it is lost in the swamps. We had driven in his four-wheel drive pick-up from Windhoek, through Otjiwarongo and Tsumeb, skirting the famous Etosha Game Reserve and across the border into Kavango where we camped for the night.

It had been a long day and a hot one but the evening was cool when the sun went down. There is no problem in finding a place to camp; thus far the road was good and the traffic negligible. There is a wide verge on each side of the road for cattle trekking on the hoof; we passed several such herds strung out and moving slowly, snatching a bite as they went, led by a small black boy with a stick and followed by another who invariably waved to us. Every twenty miles or so a sign indicated a picnic place beneath a

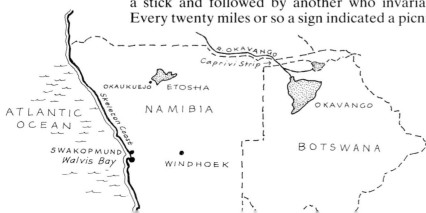

shady tree and often with a stone-built fireplace and brushwood nearby. We chose such a place well off the road and soon had a fine roaring fire and a stewpot on our iron grid. Whereas in Europe we would look for a sunny spot to picnic or camp, here one always looks for a shady tree. Water is the only problem at this season, but Reiner had a forty gallon drum of sweet well-water from his farm as well as a 200 gallon drum of petrol and enough food for a week. We were well provisioned.

We had no time to stop the truck to look at birds on our route. My companion assured me there would be more than sufficient to satisfy any ornithologist once we had passed through Ondonga and were on dirt roads with no traffic. Moreover, we would be obliged to travel slowly. Greater Kestrels were common as they perched singly on the roadside telephone poles at almost regular intervals. Sometimes a dead tree provided a perch for several ominous Vultures. This was the White-back Vulture; Reiner told me that they seem to have prescience of a calf in some herd on trek being a weakling and falling behind so that eventually it must be abandoned and would soon die from lack of water. The herd must trek from water-hole to water-hole or dam to be reached each evening; all were well known to the herdsmen; every landowner or occupier is obliged by law to give access for cattle on trek to his water supply.

Perched on the top of a termite mound by the roadside we had a good view of a Helmeted Guinea Fowl, which we were later to see in flocks at dawn seeking water. This bird was raising its blue and red helmet to utter its raucous cry.

South West Africa, now Namibia, is a sparsely populated country averaging only 1.6 persons per square mile. Kavango in the north is a native territory, from which Europeans are excluded. We had secured a South African Government permit to pass through it. The Okavango people are intelligent and industrious; I was shown the huge woven baskets in which they store the year's grain harvest for consumption and seed corn in the following year, whereas the other tribes in Kavango are improvident and keep no reserve to help them through a year of famine when the harvest fails because of drought. I was privileged

African Fish Eagle

in Orundu to see inside a chieftain's kraal which comprised eight grass huts surrounded by a thorn hedge; there were several naked children running around between the huts and women dressed in voluminous and colourful dresses who dodged hastily into their huts as we approached.

We turned east out of the town and were soon on dirt roads where the only traffic was bullock carts. As we penetrated further into the Caprivi Strip we saw no wheeled vehicles but loads on wood sledges drawn by two oxen. They had come through a long period of drought but there had been heavy rainfall two days ago and the dirt road was a quagmire. Reiner exhibited great skill in negotiating deep pools and thick mud. Lush grass and flowers were springing up. Women were working in the fields with babies slung behind their backs. The bird life was prolific.

I had my first sight of a Giant Kingfisher perched on top of a post. This is the largest of the dozen South African Kingfishers, measuring nearly half a metre in length with a long black bill. It was the male bird with white spotted plumage on a black background on the back and a red breast. This was on one of the few occasions when our vehicle was travelling at a fair speed and we came upon it suddenly; by the time we had stopped and I had my binoculars focused on it, it had decided to move. Later we had good views of the Malachite Kingfisher, a tiny bird about a third of the size of the Giant and coloured a vivid blue-green with a bright red bill. It flashed amongst the riverside trees like a jewel. Another member of this genus we saw quite often was the Pied Kingfisher, about half the size of the Giant and coloured black and white. This bird hovered above the water like a kestrel and dived when it saw a fish.

We stayed for two days at a Roman Catholic Mission run by German nuns and located on the south bank of the Okavango river. Reiner was unhappily suffering from toothache and he knew that the Mission had a lady doctor who might help to relieve it. Indeed she did by extracting the offending molar without benefit of any painkiller. Poor fellow! The extraction took her about an hour, at the end of which his face was grievously swollen. Thus we stayed an extra day which gave me a chance to

Pied Kingfisher

Reed Cormorants

go onto the river in a boat.

The river was at least a kilometre wide at this point and running very swiftly. There were crocodiles and hippopotamuses much in evidence. I was warned to give way to both of them for an annoyed hippo had a few weeks earlier bitten a large slice out of a boat. The most exciting bird I saw on the river was the African Fish Eagle perched on the branch of a large mopane tree overhanging the water. It has dark brown body and wings, a white head and chestnut belly. It plunges from its perch to catch quite big fish in its talons. Egrets and Herons were quite common. I identified the Great White Egret and the Yellow-billed Egret standing motionless on the bank but a more interesting bird for me was the African Darter.

This bird somewhat resembles a Cormorant but is more slender. We saw it several times swimming in the quieter waters of the river with its back nearly submerged and its long neck first curved backwards and then upwards and forward to carry the thin head and dagger bill. At first sight it appeared to be a snake reared up out of the water; indeed, it is often named the Snake Bird, and is thus named in Afrikaans. Its English specific name refers to its method of catching its prey – fish and frogs. It pursues them under water with its head drawn back and its neck like a coiled spring; the head darts forward and the dagger bill pierces the prey. We saw it also standing on a stone with wings spread out like a Cormorant.

We saw several Reed Cormorants which are birds of inland waters and these were always solitary amongst the reeds of small pools. These are smaller birds than the Darter and with a shorter neck; their wing span is less than that of the Cape Cormorant so common on the coast; we never saw one swimming or diving for fish and frogs on which it feeds.

On the dirt road ahead of us we saw a small group of dark-skinned people approaching us so we stopped and sat on the roadside until they came alongside. They were Bushmen with whom we could only communicate in sign language. The only man was no more than one and a half metres tall and dressed in a ragged European shirt; there were two women even less in height

Egyptian Goose

and three or four naked children. We were all very friendly; we took some photographs and gave the children a few small coins but they did not beg. The leader carried a large bracket fungus which he made clear to us would be their evening meal. These Bushmen are said to have inhabited Kavango long before the Bantu arrived from the north and to have been driven into the Kalahari desert by their more powerful neighbours.

I was surprised to see a goose perched on the very top of a great forest tree. This huge bird, measuring a metre in length, looked quite incongruous in such a position; it was black and white with a pink bill and face and pinkish legs. It was the Spurwinged Goose which has these ferocious spurs on the 'wrists' of its wings as a fighting weapon, known as the carpal spur; it is larger in the gander otherwise the two sexes look alike so I could not tell whether this was goose or gander. It remained static on its lofty perch after I had shot one hundred foot of film until my patience was exhausted.

Another goose we filmed in a creek with a following of attractive goslings was the Egyptian Goose which should more accurately have been named Egyptian Sheldgoose as it is not a true goose. They are small and colourful geese, in which the sexes are also alike. They sometimes use a ready-made nest of other waterfowl.

We were lucky to see and film a small flock of Hadeda Ibis which are rarely seen in West Africa other than in the Caprivi Strip, though common in the east. There were eight of them standing on open ground with no apparent distinction between the sexes; they are large birds with short legs and long bills less sharply curved than in the Sacred or the Glossy Ibis. They were generally dark grey in colour with a purple sheen on the wings.

I met a white South African at the Mission who had been given the task by Government to prepare a dictionary of the language of one tribe in Okavango whose language had never been written. He told me that he had collected and written down phonetically some six thousand words and had not yet finished his work. I expressed surprise that the spoken language of so primitive a people should have a rich vocabulary and had assumed that the

Swallow-tailed Bee-eater

words would all be substantive. But he denied this, saying they had words to express ideas and feelings and had different words to express different shades of meaning. I thought there must remain few opportunities left to record a language from the beginning. He said that all languages are transmitted from one generation to another through the female line and that the spoken language is a useful clue to geographical origin of a people.

The peoples of Namibia are the Ovambos, Okavango, the Herero, the Damara, the Bushmen, Hottentot and the Basters. In the Okavango area which constitutes the Caprivi Strip, there are five rather primitive tribes: Kuangari, Diriko, Hambukushu, Bunja and Sambio. In the Kalahari only the Bushmen have learned over the centuries how to survive when there may be no rain for two years, but some antelope browse on the catophractes bushes and ziziphus trees and the carnivores eat them.

We stopped on the road to admire a flock of African Quail, which are migratory, flying north in winter. Their numbers are now much reduced and the huge flocks of former times are no longer seen due to wholesale slaughter for they are good to eat. The other two species of quail in Africa suffer the same fate, the Blue Quail and the Harlequin Quail.

We reached the limit of our eastward journey where the border of Botswana was protected by a wire fence about two metres high. This is a 'Veterinary Fence' erected to protect domestic cattle against foot and mouth disease alleged to be carried by antelopes. However, a herd of elephants had recently passed that way and the fence had been pushed down and trampled flat. Elephants are no respecters of political borders; they follow their traditional migration routes and remove an obstacle in their way without apparent effort.

On our return journey we had a fine view of the Swallow-tailed Bee-eater. Unusually it was standing on the ground 'anting'. Many birds pick up ants in their bills to rub their feathers with them. The bodies contain formic acid and it is generally assumed that birds use them thus to rid themselves of parasites but I have never previously seen a Bee-eater 'anting' nor, indeed, on the ground. This particular species has a deeply forked tail and is brightly coloured like all members of its genus, mainly green and yellow with a conspicuous blue tail and a white stripe below the black face. Like other Bee-eaters it nests at the end of a metre long tunnel in a sandy bank but not colonially as does our European species.

There are few species of duck in this area despite the suitable habitat. We saw one of them which is common all over South Africa – the Red-billed Teal; it is a surface feeder in fresh water pools; the duck and the drake are similar. In the *Key to the Wildfowl of the World* it is listed as the Red-billed Pintail which is doubtless correct although it is known here as a teal. The only real teals in South Africa are the Hottentot Teal, which we saw further south in Namibia, and the Cape Teal.

Another common bird we saw for the first time here but is not seen in Europe is the Blacksmith Plover. Like other plovers it lays its eggs in a scrape on the ground but the eggs are well camouflaged and both parents guard it well and take turns in incubation. They are very wary in their approach to it, landing at some distance and only creeping to it if they think they are unobserved. This bird cannot be filmed at the nest without a hide, which has to be moved progressively nearer the nest over three days. We had not sufficient time on this occasion but elsewhere in Namibia I have filmed this handsome black and white bird on its cautious approach to the nest. Its curious name derives from its alarm call which does sound exactly like a blacksmith striking on his anvil; this is repeated many times by both sexes when there is any cause for alarm.

Two small black boys were wading barefooted in the flooded river. They appeared to be unafraid of crocodiles, hippo, iguanas, snakes or poisonous fish; but they were afraid of being photographed. I waited until they were 100 metres away and then filmed them with a telephoto lens, which did not disturb them.

We had observed such abundant bird life and seen so many new species that I felt like an alcoholic turned loose in a wine cellar. I was surfeited with birds and needed time to digest so much novelty that we motored back faster then we came.

Blacksmith = Crowned Plovers

We turned aside to spend the night at Okaukuejo in the Etosha Reserve and sat all evening in the car at a waterhole to watch the game come in to drink. First came the springbok, all females and young; very delicately they step into the water and drink, quite unafraid; maybe the buck was keeping watch nearby to raise the alarm if any predator approached. Next came a small herd of zebra – the common zebra with black stripes wider than Grevy's zebra which also lives in Namibia. Their approach is very different, noisy and excitable; they drink thirstily and deeply with much pushing and kicking; they give a high-pitched bark and are startled at the least cause for alarm. One of them had dreadful scars on its rump and back where evidently a lioness had leaped and been thrown off. Their objective appeared to be the absorption of the maximum amount of water in the shortest possible time.

There was good reason for their haste: as the shadows lengthened we heard a lion roar nearby. After a short interval a lioness appeared and then a second and a third. Finally came the lion, slowly, majestically following his pride, looking neither to left nor right, without haste and without fear. The pool was emptied of wild creatures and nothing stirred while they lapped their fill, stretched, and moved away together, they passed within three metres of our truck disdaining even a glance at it, wherein we crouched in some trepidation.

The Storks which had been roosting for hours at the very top of a nearby tree waiting until the lions had come for their evening drink, now flew down to stand in the shallow water. They were Open-billed Storks and they resembled a group of old ladies at a funeral in their black plumage and long black legs, muttering between themselves as they awaited the arrival of the corpse. They lined up close to the shore drinking and probing in the mud for any food they might have missed on the previous evening. Their curious bills have a gap about halfway in the length, possibly to emit surplus water without releasing the prey.

Precisely a quarter of an hour before sunset the Double-banded Sandgrouse, for which we had been especially waiting, began to arrive in small flocks of ten to twenty. Soon there were

Red-billed Teal

hundreds of them around the edge of the pool drinking and twittering their triple-noted call as if the social contact was more important than the biological need. As the latest birds arrived the earliest started to leave in similar groups like well-mannered cocktail party guests; as the sun sank below the skyline with a green flash all had vanished on their ten or twelve mile flight into the desert, probably carrying a load of water trapped in their breast feathers for their young waiting in the waterless area.

The great kudu came in twos and threes, looked around nervously, and plunged in up to their knees. They gulped the water quickly and scrambled out with much noise and splashing. Then appeared a family of wart hogs which had waited in the bush until the kudu left. There was a boar followed by his sow and four piglets who all trotted to the edge to drink purposefully in a disciplined manner.

The bats were flying and a Nightjar circled our truck with its beak open to trawl any insects in its flightpath. The giraffe came singly or in pairs, very silently and very alert; they spread wide their forelegs and bend the knees slightly and seemingly painfully. The long necks stretch down and they suck up the water in great draughts, of which three appear to suffice.

Last of all came the elephants moving like shadows out of the surrounding bush. First the bull to be sure all is safe and then the cows and calves. They wade deep into the water and suck it up through prehensile trunks to squirt into the open mouth. They are in no hurry for the jungle is theirs.

When the elephants had gone and the moon was up a silver-backed jackal sneaked to the water's edge like a thief in the night; it drank hastily with ears cocked.

At first light of dawn we were on our way for we had a time schedule to maintain. We had used up all our film stock before the light had failed and had no intention to stop for anything. It was, of course, ridiculous to spend only one night in the Etosha, which is best of all the African game reserves, but we had not planned it and intended to return with plenty of film stock – which we did. However, we did stop three times on our return journey.

The first was to examine through our glasses a solitary

chanting Goshawk, preening

Saddle-billed Stork. This enormous black and white bird was standing immobile and one and a half metres tall. Its excessively long legs ended in red feet and, oddly enough, its knee joints were also red. The great bill pointed down but was slightly tilted at the point; coloured black and red, it had a frontal shield of bright yellow shaped like a saddle, which gives it its name.

Before we left the reserve we were fortunate to see a hawk perched in an acacia tree quite near the road. We identified it without difficulty as the Chanting Goshawk, a beautiful name for a beautiful bird. This must surely be the loveliest of all the birds of prey, though not the noblest. Indeed, it looks more like a pigeon with its upright posture and light grey plumage. We knew this must be the Pale Chanting Goshawk because of its colour and its location in Namibia. The other species, the Dark Chanting Goshawk is found in the east. Head, breast and mantle were a lovely shade of pale grey and the belly was barred grey and white; the wing coverts were grey and the primaries black. The most striking feature was the long legs coloured a brilliant red, as was also the cere of the bill. It remained perched whilst we looked our fill and exposed some still photographs; this was probably a favourite perch from which to seize any lizard or snake killed by passing traffic. Its name derives from its musical call rising and falling in pitch, which we were not privileged to hear.

Our last stop was to watch and hear the performance of the Clapper Lark in its display flight. This is a rufous coloured lark, one of twenty three species of lark in South Africa, distinctive and interesting for its display flight which differs from our Skylark. We watched it repeat this every half-minute or so, climbing steeply to a height of about seven metres where it produces a rattling sound with its wings and then diving to a lower altitude whilst emitting a loud single whistling note. It repeats this sequence many times before returning to earth. However, its name is probably derived from the way in which it is said to 'clap' its wings as a distraction to draw an intruder away from its ground nest. This we did not see or hear.

Thinking of our Skylark at home reminded me that its display flight and song provides a perfect example of how different

en-bill and Saddle-bill Storks

observers can be impressed differently by the same event. A scientist would have recorded it in his field notes in some such words as: The male Skylark, *Alavda arvensis*, hovers above the nidification area and vocalises periodically not exceeding forty seconds. The poet wrote in his famous Ode: 'Hail to thee, blithe Spirit, bird thou never wert, that from heaven or near it poureth thy full heart in profuse strains of unpremeditated art'. And a small town boy returned from his first day in the country told a friend: 'There's this sparrer in the sky; it canna get up and it canna get down so it hangs there hollerin.'

CHAPTER THIRTEEN

The Enchanted Islands

It was Guy Mountfort who fired my ambition to visit the Galapagos Archipelago. We were attending a meeting of the British Ornithologists' Union when he told me that of all the many countries where he had watched birds this was the zenith. From that moment I started planning my visit.

That was ten years ago and the islands were not so familiar to the English public as they became after that splendid television series on the life of Charles Darwin. They lie 600 miles west of the coast of Ecuador far out in the Pacific and on the Equator. There were no commercial air flights to it and the sailings from Guayaquil had been suspended because the only ship sailing regularly to Galapagos suffered a fire on board, which put her out of commission for many months.

Fortunately I had friends in Quito and in Guayaquil who came to my rescue. They could organise three places on the Ecuadorian Airforce plane which made a weekly flight from Guayaquil to the island of Baltra, on which is the only airstrip, and that a military one built by U.S.A. during World War II. The return flight could not be reserved in advance: one had to stand by and hope that seats could be found for civilians when a plane arrived.

It would be very frustrating to spend all the time available on a single island and too risky to rely on hiring boats locally as needed; the perfect solution to our problem was to hire a power-boat complete with captain and crew and an official warden for the duration of our trip and to live on board. This I did with the help of my friends in Guayaquil: we hired a 55 foot twin-diesel-engined yacht with a steel hull and accommodation for six for three weeks.

Timing of the trip was crucial. There is only a short period when the Waved Albatross have arrived to breed on Hood island and the male Great Frigate, or Man-o'-War Bird, is still

displaying with its blown-up red gular pouch on Tower. We also hoped to see all three species of Booby feeding young and, in particular, the rare sight of about a thousand Blue-footed Boobies nesting in the volcanic crater on Daphne. The only month to accommodate all these rare spectacles is May; and so we arranged the hire for the first three weeks of May. In the event we missed the first few days but were able to add an extra week at the end. This was costly but well worthwhile.

The trip started badly but improved as it went on, which is better than the other way round. There were three of us: George and Peter and myself. We met at Heathrow Airport one hour before the flight was due to be called. We completed all formalities, checked our luggage, and waited with a pile of our binoculars, tripods, cameras, and a sound-recorder to be called. We waited and waited. Two hours after the appointed time the flight to Miami was called and we boarded with grave misgivings that our onward connections would be in jeopardy. The excuse given for the delay was the usual 'technical fault' but we knew from our unofficial sounding that it was caused by loading a spare engine for another plane grounded in U.S.A.

Although our flight schedule had left ample time to change planes at Miami, we missed the connecting flight to Quito by a few minutes and thus failed to catch the early morning flight from Quito to Guayaquil. Our friends waiting for us there were horrified to find we were not on it. They tried frantically to delay the weekly Airforce flight to Baltra in the Galapagos but, of course, we missed that too. And thus the expensive charter of our yacht began with the captain, crew and warden, who must accompany visitors on every island landing, all standing by, fuelled, watered, and provisioned, with no charterers present.

Few places are more dreary than an airport after midnight when one is waiting for an early morning flight, walking the empty marble corridors and a hundred times passing the shuttered shops. Few experiences are more frustrating than missing a plane connection by a few minutes. Few occasions when the offer of a free night's accommodation in a luxury hotel with all meals provided is rejected with such scorn. Nothing at that time can compensate for the wrecked programme and the thwarted plans. In retrospect it all sounds trivial; one learns to develop a philosophy that no trip will ever go exactly as planned so plans must be flexible. The best one should expect and hope is that more decisions will be right than wrong.

Our friends in Guayaquil did everything possible to help. We booked into a hotel in Guayaquil, which is not the city where one would choose to spend a holiday. Radio messages were sent to Baltra not to let anyone take our charter and to extend it by an extra week. They entertained us to excellent meals, secured seats for us on the next Airforce flight to Baltra – but again no guarantee we would ever return, hired for us a car, and booked us into an hotel at a seaside holiday resort a hundred miles or so distant where we could spend the inevitable wait in greater comfort and with more interest than in the hot and humid streets of Guayaquil, which lies about 100 miles up the estuary of the river Guaya and is surrounded by swamps.

We lingered four days in Playas watching sea birds but reluctant to use much film because of better things to come. There were Great Frigate Birds gliding over the tide line with their huge wings motionless or hanging over the fishing boats to swoop instantly to pick up offal thrown into the water as the fish were gutted. The females have white throats and the males a vivid red gular sack; but this was deflated and showed just as a red throat patch instead of the huge red balloon we hoped to see in the breeding territory. These birds were not feeding piratically as expected; they usually chase other sea birds, which have made a catch, until they disgorge their meal and the Frigates catch it in the air. These Frigates were just scavenging for any floating offal or edible debris.

There were a few Cowbirds flying around the palm trees and the ubiquitous Cattle Egret in the fields. A dark eagle passed overhead but it was too high for identification. The time passed slowly for there was not much to see and all preparations had been made before we set out.

We had read every book about the Galapagos we could lay our hands on. We had decided on which islands we would have the

Great Frigate Bird.

best opportunity to see which birds and the order in which we should visit them. Because of the high cost of 16 mm. colour film stock and the limited amount we could conveniently bring with us – 12,000 feet – we allocated footage to each species of bird, reptile, and mammal, with a small margin for flowers and scenery. Every night during our voyage we recorded how many feet we had shot on each subject and we kept very closely to our allocations. Once we had left the mainland we could buy no more film stock and we certainly did not intend to bring back any unexposed.

At last on May 6th we left Playas at 17.15 hours and reached the airport, where our kind friends had all assembled to see us leave. I think they wanted to be sure no hitch would delay our departure this time. We had a long wait at the airport but finally took off at 10.30. The 700 mile flight took two hours. At the airstrip on the small island of Baltra we found the warden provided by the Ecuadorian National Park Service waiting for us. To our surprise and pleasure he proved to be a young Englishman, Mike by name. Dressed only in very short shorts and with bare feet – a mode of dress he maintained throughout the voyage and at our departure – he made it clear to us that no formalities were necessary. A bus took us and all our gear to the jetty where we met Captain Pedro, an Ecuadorean, and his two local crew, one a sailor and the other a cook.

We ate lunch under an awning on deck and, still at anchor in the tiny port, we discussed with Mike and the Captain the details of our forthcoming voyage. There are forty-two islands in the archipelago besides numerous rocks and islets; only three of the islands have any inhabitants. They had planned our voyage in advance but this was to suit a typical tourist party with heaps of time for sunbathing, swimming, fishing, eating and sleeping. We had our own plans to be at the islands which were compulsory landing for us by 05.00 each morning and to remain on shore so long as the light lasted. This meant sailing between islands at night and staying more than one day on Hood and Tower, where a single day would be insufficient.

They had not had dedicated or fanatical bird watchers on board before and were somewhat taken aback at our detailed knowledge of the islands and the wildlife on each of them. Of course, we had to respect their opinion on currents, landing places and weather but we knew what we wanted to see and where we might find it.

They accepted our planned voyage with a few minor adjustments for the practicalities of sailing and landing; we reached agreement very amicably. We only varied this plan twice on the voyage, when the weather rendered it impracticable.

After lunch we made a short passage to the island named Seymour, where we saw our first Blue-footed Booby and the elegant Swallow-tailed Gull which is endemic in these islands. The small island of Mosquera is nearby; we called there to film sea-lions, although we had no lack of opportunity to film them on most of the islands later.

It is lucky for the sea-lion that it is of no commercial value or it would have suffered the fate of seals. They were hauled up on a sandy beach in great profusion, a few bulls, many cows and pups of all ages. In the mating season each bull has his own territory which he will defend vigorously from other bulls and where he rounds up his harem of cows; the pups stay with the herd until they look fully grown and rather silly as they try desperately to hang onto their mother's teats. Although they all make a great deal of noise, barking and grunting, the cows and pups are quite harmless and filled with curiosity. The bulls can be dangerous. We walked freely amongst the herd, filming them at close range and occasionally stroking a great head, which resembles that of a golden labrador.

We went aboard before darkness closed in and there we lay at anchor for some hours before sailing to Tower which is one of the most northerly islands and a long haul from Mosquera. The wind rose and the waves rose whilst our spirits sank in proportion. We retired to our bunks without supper. I remember nothing of that night except continuous retching and a blinding headache. I was told that the two crew members were also ill; only the gallant Captain Pedro was on deck to bring us safely to Tower island by 11.30 next morning.

Swallow-tailed Gull

The wind had abated and we were able to go ashore at once. Peter was still comatose so we left him in his lone bunk under the stern for another 24 hours, checking occasionally to be sure he was still breathing.

George, Mike and I climbed the rocks onto the headland and then walked across the island. The richness of bird life was a feast of good things which made us forget our nocturnal sufferings – Red-footed Boobies, Masked Boobies, and Swallow-tailed Gulls were all around us, whilst overhead sailed majestically the Magnificent Frigate Birds. Tropic Birds, Shearwaters, and Storm Petrels flew out at sea; marine iguanas and lava lizards sunned themselves on the rocks. This was what we had come so far to see and we were not disappointed.

Tower Island is also named Genovesa. All the islands are named in English and Spanish. Of course, we ought to use the Spanish word, being the language of Ecuador which owns the archipelago. So much of the exploration, however, was done by English naval vessels, whalers, and pirates that the English names have stuck, whereas some of the official Spanish names have never had universal acceptance. Thus the name by which each island is generally known to people of all nationalities, is in some instances the English name and in others the Spanish. This account of our visit employs the name in general use. Tower has another Spanish name – *Quita Sueno*, meaning Nightmare island. What horrible experience this name commemorates I could never discover.

In the evening the boat moved around to Darwin Bay on the same island where two other yachts were already anchored; but their passengers did not come ashore. This is a very sheltered bay where we had a good night's rest and were ready for serious and organised filming next morning. We landed on a sandy beach at dawn and soon located the breeding colony of Frigate Birds. This includes both the Magnificent Frigate Bird and the Great Frigate Bird, which are very similar; the latter, whose scientific name is *Fregata minor* is also named the Man-o'-War bird.

Here is a fantastic sight we could have watched for hours. The females are more readily distinguishable than the males, the

Great having a white belly, throat and chin, whilst the Magnificent females have a black throat patch. They floated on their enormous 2.4 metre wing span close above the scalesia bushes, whereon crouched awkwardly the males of both species with their fantastic red gular pouches inflated to great balloons, on which they rested their long hooked bills. The air was filled with excited cries as the male birds tried to attract the attention of the discerning females to their splendid balloonery. The birds were too interested in their own love affairs to pay any attention to us; all too soon we had used up our total allocated footage.

There were many young birds too, hopping about the low bushes, which were brown rather than black. Adults and juveniles alike clung awkwardly with tiny feet to twigs bent under their weight; the toes are not webbed, as one might expect of a marine bird, but divided to grip the branches during their short time ashore each year. These birds are essentially aerial, alighting very rarely on land or water but circling and gliding on the air currents until they display the speed and power of their flying ability in piratical chases of a Booby with a fish in its gizzard or a sudden swoop to pick up edible flotsam from the sea.

We found a Yellow-crowned Night Heron picking its way delicately amongst the pools. It usually feeds at night so we were lucky to find it hunting for crabs in the early morning, which made filming possible.

We walked along the cliff edge until we reached the trig point shown on our map and there turned inland and uphill to find the crater. We climbed for two hours over boiler plates of lava and through the dense scalesia bushes without success. The sun was very hot and the rocks burned under our rubber shoes. We decided that there were many more craters of inactive volcanoes to be found more easily and so returned to our boat and a welcome lunch.

This day set the gastronomic pattern for the future. We breakfasted early and heartily after a morning swim. Having sailed in the late evening or overnight, we found ourselves at every dawn save two, anchored close to a new island. So we were eager to be ashore just as soon as the light was good enough to expose film. Lunch would be on board at any time in the afternoon when hunger or excessive heat or exhaustion of the film stock taken ashore prevailed over our desire to see more birds. We fed on deck under an awning; the food was excellent or our appetites made it seem so. Our cook was ingenious; he produced gallons of thirst-quenching liquid by liquidising fruits of all kinds. There was always a huge 'help yourself' branch of bananas on deck, to which we paid our respects many times a day.

It amused me to see the cook inspect this each morning to tear off and throw into the sea any fruit which gave the slightest hint of being over-ripe. The branch burdened with hundreds of bananas was renewed frequently during the voyage. Another bonus from the munificence of the environment was lobster. Whenever anchored in two or three fathoms, our sailor would dive overboard once a day, swim underwater without any aqualung and presently bring up a large lobster. Thus fresh lobster was a staple of our diet and we dined as luxuriously as in the best restaurant.

After a quick lunch we landed again but this time on the steep rocks on the east side of the bay. We split up so that George could concentrate on filming Red-footed Boobies and I on Masked Boobies, whilst Peter took still photos and Mike did some sound recording.

The three species of Booby endemic in the Galapagos – Blue-footed, Red-footed, and Masked are closely related to our Gannet of the northern seas. There are three more species of Booby in the genus – the Peruvian, the Brown and the Abbot's – distribution in tropical seas is world-wide. The Masked, which I was filming on Tower, is the largest species of the genus, all white except for its black face, orange eyes and bill, and green legs and feet. The mask gives it an incognito look.

Sailors christened these large sea birds Booby because they were stupid to allow themselves to be so easily caught and killed on land. The closely related Gannet is named by French sailors *Fou de Bassin*, which could be translated port idiot! This confirms the unwarranted reputation for folly.

In the glossary to Masefield's *Salt-water Ballads* the name

Yellow-crowned Night Heron

Molleymak is applied to the Fulmar petrel. This is derived from the Dutch name for the same bird, *Mallemok* meaning a stupid gull. The Guillemot is often called the 'foolish Guillemot'; and that superb navigator and aviator, the Albatross, is called by Masefield a 'Goney', which should read 'Gony' and is from the root of 'Goon' – a 'stupid fellow'; I believe the Japanese refer to all three species found in their waters as *Bakadori* or 'fool bird'.

This general attribute of folly to most large sea birds must surely derive from sailors' comparison to their own craftiness.

In the Galapagos, Boobies are breeding and feeding young from October to June and may be found on Tower, Hood and Daphne islands when not at sea diving for fish in the tropical waters. For the remaining three months they are not seen at all on the islands. Off the west coast of South America they may be seen streaming past ships in tens of thousands as they make their way to or from the rich fishing grounds of the Humboldt current.

Sadly their numbers have recently been depleted because these waters have been severely over-fished by fleets of trawlers to feed the government-sponsored fish-meal factories. The product was chiefly exported for fertiliser and the desire to earn more foreign exchange so reduced the vast shoals of anchovy that millions of sea birds have had to starve; the trawlers' rich harvests dwindled to an uneconomic level, and the fish-meal factories were closed. Recently I saw in several west coast ports twenty to thirty derelict trawlers in each port rusting away. Sic transit gloria mundi!

From the top of the high cliff we watched and filmed an endless procession of sea birds flying below us – Boobies and Pelicans, Frigates and Tropic Birds. The latter flew singly and purposefully with steadily flapping wings in a straight line, returning from the feeding ground where they dive for fish. This is a very beautiful bird, pure white with two long tail feathers streaming out behind and a brilliant red bill. George was fortunate to find a hen bird sitting on its single egg in a hole in the volcanic rock. The tip of its tail feather just showed at one end of the hole and its vivid beak was only a short way inside the other so that we were able to observe it at very close quarters. It appeared to be unafraid but gave Mike's finger a severe peck for coming too close.

I was recording less exciting subjects when George filmed an unusual and rather tragic event. A Wedge-rumped Petrel emerged from its nest in a hole in the rock and was seized by a Lava Gull which had been waiting for this delectable prey. The cannibalistic gull seized the petrel in its bill and proceeded to batter it on the rock for some minutes and then to swallow it whole. Not a pleasant sight!

It was here we saw our first marine iguanas but we saw them on every island we visited except on Floriana. On Hood, far to the south, they have evolved differently in that they have a red coloration on the back instead of being uniformly grey as on other islands. They are ferocious-looking reptiles but quite harmless. They resemble small dragons with a row of dorsal spines and vicious jaws, but are vegetarian, feeding on seaweed. Soon after dawn and again in the evening they clamber down from the rocks and swim in shallow water to feed. On return to shore they hastily climb over the rocks and often ascend steep cliffs to attain a position in which to gain full benefit from the rising sun. It is for this ascent that they have powerful claws and we marvelled at the precarious pinnacles they could climb.

In a sunny spot they pack closely together to conserve heat and they harmonise wonderfully with the lava rock. There they lie motionless for hours to absorb the heat of the sun, only moving to receive the sun's rays more directly. It seems to be their main object in life after feeding to raise their body temperature, whereas the land iguanas, which we found later on South Plaza and Fernandina, are sporadic and pass the heat of the day in their earth burrows to avoid undue rise in temperature. The marine iguana ejects excess salt through the nostrils in a fine spray.

On our return to the boat by dinghy we saw Storm Petrels as well as more Wedge-rumped Petrels, and also Audubon's Shearwaters skimming the tops of the waves. We left Tower soon after midnight whilst we were fast asleep and only our gallant captain navigated to Bartholomew, which we reached at eight o'clock the following morning. Here we did climb up to the crater. The islands are all of volcanic origin rising from the ocean bed where there is a shelf which connects to Costa Rica; there is much greater depth between the Galapagos and South America, the ocean bed dropping steeply to a thousand fathoms off the west coast of the continent.

We rowed the dinghy along the rocky coast and in a cave we saw our first Galapagos Penguin. They are small stocky birds which stand upright on the rock and jump into the water. They measure only thirty centimetres in length and have the usual black and white penguin colouring. No other species of this large genus is found so far north; it is quite astonishing to find this cold water bird living and breeding on the Equator. It is, of course, endemic in the Galapagos and found on the shores of four islands in the west of the archipelago. They exhibited no fear so that we were able to film their quaint appearance and spasmodic movements quite easily from the boat.

It is one of the many wonders of these islands to be able to watch penguins associated with the Antarctic and flamingos associated with the tropics on the same day. Later we found a penguin breeding site on Fernandina where they nest in holes in the lava rock at the sea's edge. They jumped clear from the water right into their holes: but George was able to take one in his hand; it was the size of a puffin and very plump. The feeding must be good.

We sailed on to nearby James Island, which is named in Spanish, San Salvador. It is a much larger island which formerly had a few inhabitants who processed salt mined in the volcanic crater. The derelict buildings and remains of machinery were a hideous sight amid such surroundings. The operators had pulled out without making any attempt to clear up the mess they had made.

We called in at Buccaneer Cove with its sheer rock cliffs and its great Pinnacle Rock from which buccaneers and pirates kept watch for potential victims to attract or ships of the Royal Navy to avoid. Then we hove to at an excellent anchorage in James Bay and put the dinghy ashore on the Espumilia beach. This is bordered by a thick screen of scalesia trees, beyond which are two lagoons of brackish water where I filmed the White-cheeked Pintail. A juvenile Striated Heron was wandering on its own along the beach and two fur seals were swimming in a rocky pool connected to the sea under a bridge of rock. Great numbers of these animals were killed during the nineteenth century for their valuable skins. Until recently this species was considered extinct, no specimen having been observed for many years. A few years ago, however, a small colony was located and now they are fully protected by law and increasing in number. Their movement in the water is superbly graceful.

We had our first sight here of the Large-billed Flycatcher, sometimes named the Tyrant Flycatcher. This is a slender brown and yellow bird about fifteen centimetres in length and thus larger than but not so startling in colour as the only other flycatcher in the islands, the Vermilion. Like so many of the birds here it is endemic. Another endemic bird, of which we had our first sighting on James, is the Galapagos Hawk, which is well dispersed throughout the archipelago but now much reduced in numbers. It was perched on a tree and showed no alarm at our approach. Mike made a good sound recording of its strident screech. As we did not immediately retire it flew at me in a long effortless glide and knocked my hat off my head. Maybe it resented me keeping my head covered in its presence! It is a large dark-brown bird which feeds on smaller birds and lizards. It is one of the few animal predators which help to preserve the balance of living creatures. Although described as a hawk, it is in fact a species of buzzard.

Man himself was the most dangerous predator. He and the animals he introduced intentionally or unknowingly have extinguished some species and endangered others. Occasional ships of buccaneers and more regular visits of whalers allowed their crews to land for fresh water and to collect the giant tortoise for fresh meat.

Rats came ashore from the ships and caused devastation to many species of wild life, especially by preying on young tortoises to such an extent that scientists could find no young tortoises nor rear any until they provided protected areas for the young up to four years of age.

Dogs, cats and pigs landed as pets or food all ran wild to cause

Galapagos Hawk

havoc amongst the local animals and plants. But perhaps the worst offenders are the goats landed on some uninhabited islands. These grazed and browsed so efficiently and multiplied so fast that they eliminated all competitive animals and most of the plant life. It is recorded that two pairs of goats were landed on Pinta island in 1959 with the object of providing a source of fresh meat for fishermen in that area. Some twenty years later it was noticed that the island was being defoliated and it was decided to make a significant cull. 40,000 goats were shot, by which time the survivors had become too wary to approach within range. Too many were left to guarantee revival of the vegetation and a cull will be needed at regular intervals, which is no bad prospect for those who like goat meat.

Before the arrival of man, the birds, reptiles and mammals lived in the state of innocence that presumably existed in the Garden of Eden before the fall of Adam. The aboriginal creatures lived in harmony until the ecological balance was destroyed by man's thoughtless introduction of exotic species.

After watching a Green Heron picking its way delicately along the shore-line and making occasional hurried but unsuccessful dashes to spear a small fish, we returned on board for a meal and sleep. Soon after midnight the Captain and crew raised the anchor and set a course for Tagus Bay on the island of Isabella. At dawn next morning we heard the engine cut when Mike roused us to witness a thrilling sight we would not have wished to miss.

Hurrying on deck, we were amazed to find ourselves in the midst of a pod of sperm whales. These huge mammals, about the length of our boat, were all around us, rolling to the surface, slapping the water with enormous flukes, spouting and sounding. Had they exhibited any animosity or signs of fear, we should have been alarmed: a single blow from a fluke would have smashed our small craft; but they appeared to be so relaxed at play that we were not afraid. At times these enormous beasts lay quiescent on the surface presenting a great brown shining back close to our boat. In the presence of such benevolent power we felt humble and ashamed of our fellow humans who could wreak such havoc with their exploding harpoons. Nineteenth century whaling almost brought the sperm whale to extinction whereas a late eighteenth century sea captain has described a migration of sperm whale passing through the antipodes in an unbroken line from earliest dawn to dusk.

As we drifted apart from the pod, our sailor started up the engine and we pursued our course to Tagus Bay. After landing there we scrambled along the rocky shore where Brown Pelicans were nesting on low bushes close to the water. The nest was a platform of twigs poised precariously on the top of these bushes, and seemingly very slight for so large a bird. The hen birds continued to incubate their two or three white eggs without any sign of alarm, whilst I filmed at a distance of only three metres.

Seen thus at close quarters and in breeding plumage this ungainly and rather drab bird is very beautiful around the head and neck. The lower mandible supports a very flexible sack which can hold a sizable catch of fish preparatory to swallowing. The Pelicans in Africa sometimes fish in shallow water as a team which surrounds a shoal of fish and drives it to the centre with massive resultant catches. I never saw the Brown Pelicans of the Pacific fish in this fashion but only to fly along the coast and suddenly hurl themselves headlong and clumsily into the water on sighting a shoal. On emerging they floated for a few moments on the surface with water running out of the closed bill and a flurry of Brown Noddies noisily grabbing any fish which escaped from the capacious lower mandible.

The female birds on the nest engaged in a marital display by occasionally snapping their huge bills at the male birds sailing majestically overhead on idle wings.

It was on this island that we had our first view of another bird unique to these islands – the Flightless Cormorant. This is the only species in a wide-spread and ancient family, which has lost the power of flight. It is thought that there can be no more than 800 pairs of this sombre bird and it is not seen beyond the confines of its breeding areas on Fernandina and Isabella islands. Indeed, until quite recently it was thought to be yet another extinct species. It dives to feed on bottom fish, eels and octopus; in consequence it is in perpetual danger of being caught underwater wherever fishermen set lobster pots and fish traps.

We filmed a pair engaged in an elaborate courtship display both on the rock and in the water. They circle each other in a gracious minuet with frequent bowing and the accompaniment of a low growling sound. The dull brown plumage of this curious bird seems to have degenerated (or evolved?) until it is more like hair than feathers and lacks the metallic sheen of other species of Cormorant. It is a powerful swimmer under water, for which it is equipped with four webbed toes on each foot. The only relief from the uniform dark brown colour is the flesh-coloured bill tip.

We sailed out of Tagus Bay on a Sunday morning after breakfast to make the short crossing to Fernandina. It was in this area that the sailing ship of an early navigator was once becalmed whilst a volcano on Fernandina erupted. As the hot lava flowed into the sea, its temperature rose alarmingly until the pitch between the ship's planks began to melt and run out. The captain and crew thought that all was lost but luckily a slight wind arose which enabled them to make sail and clear the area just in time. That was probably the last eruption of Wolf volcano.

We landed on Fernandina at a peninsula which was all mangrove swamp and shallow pools in the lava rock. Here were many sea-lions in most playful mood; one was chasing a marine iguana and nipping its tail. The iguana swam frantically in its effort to escape but the sea-lion could overtake it with a single swirl of a flipper to give it another nip. The iguana was in no danger because sea-lions do not eat them; but the iguana was not to know this. Another clambered into our dinghy and seemed to be interested in the outboard engine. As we rushed to the dinghy to avert any damage being done, it dived neatly overboard. They are the most friendly and curious of creatures, rather like yellow retrievers. Though about the same size as the fur seal, they have a more canine muzzle and a distinguishable neck; their fur is not nearly so dense as that of the seal. As night falls we hear them barking and snorting all around us.

We walked inland over ribbon lava which is also named rope lava. The shapes and patterns of flowing lava are very diverse and

I wonder what freaks of temperature and wind cause it to solidify into such strange shapes of tube and slab. I understand that flowing lava cooled rapidly forms flat slabs and when cooled slowly is contorted and broken. A Yellow Warbler was singing its very sweet but feeble song of a few thin notes. It is the only .resident warbler and is widespread throughout the Archipelago. Many of them must have been blown by hurricane winds from the east since these islands rose from the seabed.

One of the delights of the rocky pools on the shore-line is the Sally Lightfoot crab which abounds in great numbers and a variety of sizes, according to age. Their shells are a vivid red which darkens as they grow older and bigger. They appear to skim across the surface of the pools but whether or not an odd leg extended to the bottom helps them over, I never could see. There are many different species of fiddler crabs, hermit crabs and ghost crabs, but our absorbing interest is in birds so we passed them by. Peter, who is a marine biologist, however, made the point that little work has yet been done on the marine life of the islands. It should be conserved with the same thoroughness by the Ecuadorian National Park Service so that the biological integrity of each island is not violated and unique species in danger of extinction are protected. It is as important to harmonise the marine ecosystem with human pressures as the land.

A visitor to one island a century ago took a very jaundiced view of what he saw. He recorded his impression in somewhat morbid terms:

'Behind a dilapidated pier and ramshackle huts stretched miles of dreary greyish-brown thorn bush, on most parts dense but sparser where a recent lava flow had turned the ground into a slag heap. The land rose gradually with no exciting features to a sordid cultivated region, beyond which, partly concealed in cloud, were green downs.

'The biological peculiarities are offset by an enervating climate, monotonous scenery, dense thorn scrub, cactus spines, loose sharp lava, food deficiencies, water shortage, black rats, fleas, jiggers, ants, mosquitoes, scorpions, Indians of doubtful honesty, and dejected disillusioned European settlers.'

My own impressions were very different. The islands have a special beauty of their own. Only three out of the forty-two islands have any inhabitants at all and these are sparse. The worst that man can do to vilify nature is scarcely noticeable, and most of it has been cleared up under the excellent management as a nature reserve of international importance. The above defamatory words were probably written about a single visit to one bay on one island, Santa Cruz, where was for a short while established a penal settlement.

To me the islands all have different facets of beauty, some primitive, some mysterious, some magical. The sea is turquoise or sapphire, or emerald, according to its depth and what lies under it. The waves break white on jagged rocks or lap lazily upon a sandy beach. The rocks are black except where whitened by the accumulation of bird droppings over thousands of years. The beaches may be yellow, or white, or black, red or green according to the chemistry of the sand. Some islands rise sheer from the ocean, being the steep sides of a volcano, others are the broken edges of ancient craters, weathered by wind and sea into fantastic pinnacles and arches. On others you may land on a lava flow congealed in amazing patterns as if just yesterday. The colour here is a uniform grey but relieved wherever a crack or crevice will allow the vivid green of opuntia cactus with its bright yellow blossom and the fleshy leaves of the cryptocarcus.

These islands are the tops of mountains risen to one thousand five hundred metres from the mid-oceanic ridge a million years ago. Some have subsided since the original submarine upheaval and others have been lifted up relative to earlier levels. Inland there is a narrow arid belt and then a humid zone, rich in vegetation. On the higher islands where mountains rise four thousand feet above sea-level, grow tall forest trees; above that tree belt is another arid zone where only cactus grows.

On a few shores a mangrove swamp has been able to establish with stilt roots and there are colonies of other birds.

In the coastal arid zone between the flows of grey wrinkled lava there may be plains of sultry red volcanic ash where the only living thing is the rare brachycercus cactus. Behind this and sheltered by a grove of silvery palo santo trees may lie a lagoon of brackish water, the winter quarters of numerous migrant waders from the north and, if one is lucky, the lovely sight of pink Flamingos.

Looking down from a hill of soft turf one may see in shallow aquamarine water many craters, large and small, beneath the clear waves. Beauty is everywhere, sometimes gentle and quiet but more often stark and vivid. It is always arresting and ever to be remembered.

We sailed from Fernandina at 02.00 on a Monday morning, and, although we were blissfully unaware of it, there was a strong southerly head wind so we made slow progress south east to James Island. We dropped anchor in James Bay on that island at 14.30 hours and found another small boat out of Santa Cruz already there. However, its crew and passengers, including several children, showed no intent to go ashore and thus we had the island to ourselves as usual. Odd how people will travel so far and have no curiosity to see the wonders that await them at their destination.

We landed immediately by dinghy and followed a path which led us through beautiful grottos. Amongst the lava were deep emerald sea-water pools fed by tunnels in the rock, and quaint bridges of lava over the open channels. This is said to be a favourite haunt of the Galapagos fur seal, but we saw only five of this rare species, two adults and three half-grown pups. They were all very lethargic and our proximity worried them not at all. A young sea-lion pup was in more playful mood and it was a joy to watch its sinuous movements in shallow water. A Yellow-crowned Night Heron stepped delicately along the edges of the pools.

Returning along the shore-line, we saw many waders, migrants from the north, and shy by comparison with the endemic fauna. The Whimbrel with its long curved bill and prominent eye-stripe breeds in the circumpolar Arctic and it was good to see it here in its winter quarters. The Oystercatcher was there too, in its black and white livery and with its long orange bill which always looks too heavy. The shrill calls of these two familiar birds brought thoughts of home. The Semi-palmated Plover was less familiar but easily identified as a North American bird and new to us as also was the Wandering Tattler.

We sailed overnight and dawn found us at anchor off the small island of Jervis to the south of Santa Cruz. We landed from the dinghy at 06.30, after a hasty breakfast, to look for the birds we had come to this island especially to see. The beach here is a vivid red of volcanic ash and above it is a belt of pale green cryptocarcus bushes with fleshy leaves. Pushing our way through these we reached the edge of a wide lagoon of brackish water, several hectares in extent, and shimmering in the early morning sun. And there, as we had hoped, was a large flock of Flamingos only a hundred metres distant.

We used extreme caution in setting up our tripods in the shelter of the trees for Flamingos are shy birds which have a way of moving as a flock away from any disturbance without any panic but maintaining always the same intervening distance. We had no desire to narrow that distance for our variety of telescopic and zoom lenses could bring their image as close as we could wish.

The farther shores were clad with palo santo trees, leafless at this season and rising, as we judged, to about six metres. Their silvery-grey trunks and branches made a fitting background to the brilliant colouring of the feeding flock. These were the Greater Flamingo (*F. rubis*), red and white with black wing tips. The red had an orange tinge and the colour was vivid, indicating a good food supply. They kept together as a flock in a depth of water up to their ankle joints. All their long and flexible necks were extended down into the water to reach the muddy bottom with their huge bills. These weave to and fro rythmically as they sift the muddy water through the sieves within their mandibles to extract the tiny invertebrates and shrimps on which they feed.

When we had watched our fill and exposed our full allocation of film (plus a little extra we could not resist for close-ups of the head and bill) we withdrew as quietly as we had come. We sailed at 08.30 for the largest and most inhabited island, Santa Cruz, and made our landfall in Conway Bay with Eden Isle lying just offshore. This is on the west side of Santa Cruz and hence remote from the tiny port of Academy Bay. We called here particularly to see the land iguanas which are becoming scarce. We saw only one approaching us like a benevolent dragon but it turned and fled at the sight of us and took refuge in its burrow. Mike assured us we would have a better chance to film this species on South Plaza. There is an attractive lagoon on shore fringed with mangrove but we saw no birds on it. Elsewhere there were stands of opuntia cactus alive with finches and Mocking Birds. There are four species of Mocking Bird in the islands and this one was the most common, the Galapagos Mocking Bird. It is a dull-plumaged bird with a bright eye and insatiable curiosity. No problem here to come within close-up distance to film; the problem is to keep the Mocking Bird far enough away to take a picture. They would perch on the cameras, the tape recorder or our shoulders and seemed reluctant to let us go.

The finches are known collectively as Darwin Finches and that careful observer identified thirteen separate species. To the observer in the field they are not too dissimilar but it is their size, the shape and size of their bills and their feeding habits which are diagnostic. It was Darwin's theory that all are descended from a common ancestor and that their selection of a particular eco-logical niche for feeding and breeding has developed their individual physical features to exploit that niche to maximum advantage. Thus he developed his world-shaking theory of *The Origin of Species by Means of Natural Selection*. It was here we watched the Cactus Finch with its powerful, elongated and slightly curved bill feeding on the fruit of the prickly pear cactus. It invariably makes its nest in a hole excavated in the fleshy trunk of the same plant.

Separate species have developed on the more distant islands, beyond easy flying distance. One of the most interesting is the Woodpecker Finch which has been observed to select a twig or cactus spine, break it to the required length, and hold it in its bill to probe a crevice and extract an insect beyond the reach of its long bill. We did not witness this astonishing act of inherited wisdom: it is alleged to have taken the ancestors of Man a few million years to acquire the art of making and using tools.

Woodpecker Finch

Other species of Darwin's finches which we should have found on various islands and identified from the shape of their bills are:

Large Ground Finch black and very heavy bill
Medium Ground Finch
Small Ground Finch
Sharp-billed Ground Finch
Cactus Finch   black colour – pointed bill
Large-billed Cactus Finch
Vegetarian Finch   yellow colour finch bill
Parrot-billed Finch   black colour parrot bill
Medium Tree Finch black colour finch bill
Small Tree Finch
Woodpecker Finch   fawn colour long bill
Mangrove Finch
Warbler Finch   reddish and very fine
                      pointed bill

We identified only five of these species.

We sailed by night around the southern end of Santa Cruz and up the east coast to Academy Bay, which one might regard as the metropolis of the Galapagos, having a Government presence in a Customs official and a military representative. Here live a few permanent inhabitants engaged in fishing or farming or hiring boats to visitors and a number of temporary dwellers who work at the Darwin Research Station. This international organisation is financed in the main from U.S.A. and Europe and staffed by scientists from both areas on a rota basis.

Naturally we made this our first call and presented our credentials to the Director, to whom we had an introduction. We handed over a small consignment of bird rings with which we had been entrusted from U.K., and some coloured slides of moths from Roger Perry. These assignments being fulfilled, we were shown around the laboratories and workshops and the Tortoise House.

The Galapagos tortoise, after which the whole archipelago is named, is endemic and nearly unique, being one of the two giant tortoises in the world, the other being on Aldabra in the Indian Ocean. When Charles Darwin made his famous visit here in 1835, he was able to distinguish thirteen separate and identifiable sub-species living on different islands. Three of these have since become extinct and a fourth on the island of Pinta had been reduced to a solitary male animal. It, too, would have been the last of its sub-species had not a female of the same species happily been located in the San Diego Zoo which has since been returned to the Research Station for breeding to save the race. Twenty-seven young have now been hatched, reared and returned to Hood island, so this doomed race is saved.

This herbivorous and harmless reptile was once so plentiful on most of the islands that pirates, buccaneers, whalers and mer-chantmen called there for fresh water and what the English sailors named 'Galapagos mutton'. It is estimated that more than 100,000 were taken by easy capture over the centuries. The crews would turn them over onto their carapace and then drag them to the ship where they were packed alive in layers in the hold. Devoid of food and water and with a minimum of air they could survive for as long as six months and thus provide fresh meat to the crews. This slaughter nearly extinguished an almost unique reptile.

When the Institute decided to save it, there remained only an estimated 1,500 to 2,000 left in the islands. All the sub-species are now totally protected and there is a tortoise reserve on Santa Cruz to safeguard the young from rats and other introduced predators and to provide ideal breeding and feeding conditions for the most endangered sub-species. When we were there, 600 young tortoises of ten different sub-species had been hatched and reared.

Those reduced to a dangerously low level are further helped by wardens collecting eggs from Pinta and Hood to be hatched in incubators at the Research Station. The young are reared in safety up to the age of five years when they are returned to the island from which the eggs were taken. Subsequent checks on the numbered carapaces have shown a hundred percent survival rate so that there is good hope that ten sub-species will survive.

The sub-species are divided into two main races. Those on Duncan Island and Albermarle have 'saddleback' carapaces which allow the reptile to raise its head and stretch its long neck to enable it to feed on the fleshy leaves of the opuntia cactus. On all other islands the local sub-species have domed carapaces and they feed at ground level. The surviving tortoises are most numerous on Albermarle and Santa Cruz. They all lay their eggs in deep soil and cover them over to hatch. The largest and oldest living in mountainous areas have carapaces pitted with small holes; it has been suggested that these have been caused by hot cinders from erupting volcanoes which would confirm their alleged longevity.

The hatching success rate is ninety-five percent and incubation takes six months. A further small loss in very early life leaves a success rate of ninety percent before being returned to their islands when they are big enough to be immune to depredation by rats.

The different sub-species, each peculiar to its island, are kept in separate enclosures to avoid any possibility of cross-breeding. Small arid islands produce the smaller sub-species and the larger and more lush islands the larger.

The common belief that this reptile will live for four hundred years has not been scientifically substantiated. But the largest and therefore oldest specimen at the Research Station is believed to be over 200 years old, and it weighs 450 pounds. It moves slowly and inexorably like a tank.

A beautiful bird we hoped to see is the male Vermilion Flycatcher. As its name implies it is a bright vermilion in colour whereas its mate is a bright yellow. It was our intention to see and film both. We knew we should need to reach above the tropical zone to find them and were advised to start our search at a tiny hamlet named Bella Vista. Surprisingly there is a form of public transport in Santa Cruz, a single and ancient bus which connects the few hamlets on the island with the small port in Academy Bay. We were fortunate to find it running on that day in the direction we wanted. The only other passenger was a farmer of Norwegian origin, one of the few colonists who had stayed the course. My smattering of Norwegian encouraged his natural friendliness and we were soon on excellent terms. Some Nor-

wegian and German settlers arrived in 1920 to cultivate banana
and sugar plantations but few remained.

As the bus climbed up on a primitive road through the humid
zone we noted the changing vegetation – tree ferns, elephant
grass, bamboo, balsa, papya and thence into the 'Highlands' with
scattered and stunted trees in a verdant parkland. At Bella Vista
we all alighted, and having ascertained at what hour it would
leave for Santa Cruz, and at his invitation, we set off on a walk
with the Norwegian to his farm, he carrying his load of purchases
and we our photographic equipment. He told us that he was
familiar with the Vermilion Flycatcher and could show us where
we would be likely to find it. For this we were most grateful, for
the bird is only the size of a sparrow and forages singly or in pairs
so that finding it in a vast area might have taken a long time.

On approaching his house we were greeted by the barking of
several dogs and a pack of Alsatians rushed at us and greeted him
joyously – without his presence I doubt if our reception by them
would have been so friendly! He explained that he kept so many
to protect his crops from the wild pigs that abound in the island –
another relic of the introduction of an exotic species which had
proved to be a mistake. However, his dogs fed well on pork and
he shot a pig whenever he wanted pork or bacon as a change of
diet.

Leaving his load at the farm, he led us upward for about a mile
through his pastures and presently we saw a female Flycatcher on
the trunk of a tree hung with epiphytes. She had a bright yellow
breast and the rest of her plumage was brown. Soon we located
the male bird and we had ample opportunity to study and film him
as he flitted among low bushes. His feeding habits are dissimilar
to either of the species of Flycatcher familiar to us in Europe – the
Spotted Flycatcher which always flies from a favourite perch and
takes its prey in the air and the Pied Flycatcher which forages on
the ground. His head and breast are a very brilliant red with a
black eye-stripe and his back and tail are strongly contrasting
black. We returned to the farm well satisfied with our filming to
thank the farmer for his help. He introduced his wife who
appeared to speak only Norwegian and they insisted on us having

Vermilion Flycatcher

a drink with them.

We walked back down the hill to Bella Vista and caught the bus which did not return directly but went to a higher group of houses named Santa Costa at about 600 metres above sea level, beyond which the driver kindly stopped to allow us to look down into an extinct volcanic crater about 200 metres deep.

Our next island was Floriana which is a large island at the southern latitude of the Archipelago and one of the three which has a few inhabitants. There were estimated to be between four and five thousand inhabitants divided between all the islands, of which the larger proportion is on San Cristobel. We landed at Punta Cormorant where the beach has a greenish tinge due to the presence of olivaceous crystals. There were three other yachts at anchor in the bay, but no one going ashore; one was flying the Japanese flag. We rowed the dinghy a short distance out to sea into a submerged crater of an extinct volcano. Most of the broken rim of this crater juts out of the sea like a jagged tooth which urgently requires the attention of a dentist. We took our boat through a gap in the rim into the calm water inside. This is known as the Devil's Crown and we had hoped to see Tropic Birds here but none were flying. There was some vegetation which had found a root hold on the precipitous and ragged edge of the crater, which I was told was jasminocernis.

On shore at Floriana we found a salt water lagoon with a flock of twenty-one Flamingos. Their colouring varied from salmon pink to orange, probably with the age of the bird. This is one of only three islands on which the species – the Greater Flamingo – may be found and then only when the salinity is absolutely right for them. So we were lucky to see them here and on Jervis. The total Flamingo population of Galapagos is five hundred to one thousand birds. Along the shore of this lagoon we filmed a variety of migrant waders feeding, the Whimbrel, the Stilt, the Semi-palmated Plover, the Lesser Yellowlegs and the Ruddy Turnstone. This latter is a gay harlequin of a bird, brighter in colour than our European species. It breeds within the Arctic circle and winters in South America, whereas our European species also breeds in the Arctic but winters in Europe and as far away as

South Africa. Characteristically, it was running along the shore line with quick spasmodic movements and flipping over quite large stones with its bill to look for tiny marine animals underneath.

Further along the coast there is an inlet which has been known for a century or two as Post Office Bay. On shore is a post with a barrel nailed to it, into which mariners could insert mail to any part of the world without the necessity of postage stamps with a fair chance of them being ultimately delivered. This practice still continues. We recalled how, until the introduction of radio, the lonely islanders of St Kilda had found the most reliable means of communication with the mainland was to put a written message in a sealed bottle and fasten it securely to a wooden float. They attached a blown-up sheep's bladder and a piece of rag to act as a flag and launched this into the Atlantic when a strong west wind was blowing. These were picked up in the Outer Hebrides, or on the mainland of Scotland, and even in Norway, when the missive was eventually delivered to the addressee. Evidently a high percentage of these communications were received safely. It is to the credit of the public that they accept an obligation to forward such messages as survive a hazardous journey.

The sea was too rough to permit a landing at Post Office Bay as we had hoped, so we missed the opportunity to leave letters for England which would be treasured by our philatelic friends if they bore any evidence of being posted here; and we missed the chance to test the efficiency of this voluntary mail service, as well as to walk up to one or more of the extinct volcanoes there. There are eighty craters on this island, an average of one per square mile. One can imagine the fury of sight and sound when several of these were active at one time.

We sailed on to another potential landing place named Black Beach and hoped the wind would abate. Mike told us that there is there a rest house which provides meals which have the reputation of being very edible and a welcome change from the normal seafarers' food. He had taken the precaution to radio the proprietor a few days earlier with a request to prepare a particularly large and delicious dinner for us. On the way we saw large areas of ocean covered with what we took to be a huge oil slick and we were bemoaning the pollution caused by modern shipping even in this remote part of the Pacific Ocean. However, Captain Pedro told us this was plankton, source of nourishment of krill, a minute form of shrimp found in billions in Antarctic seas and the basic food of some species of whales, brought from thence by the Humboldt current.

In anticipation of our splendid meal ashore we all shaved and changed out of our usual garb of shorts or bathing trunks into more civilised clothing. We anchored at Black Beach and all climbed into the dinghy except Captain Pedro who valued his ship more than a good dinner. But the swell was too great and the breakers too fierce for our heavily laden dinghy to make the passage through them to the beach. Time and again she was nearly swamped until we accepted the fact that there was no way to reach the shore, so tantalisingly close, except by swimming. It was not worthwhile to ruin our only decent clothing even for a good dinner and so we reluctantly put back to the boat. By the time we came on board it was nearly dark and the Captain decided that with the rising wind the anchor would drag and we must try to reach a sheltered anchorage. Fortunately, it was a clear night with a quarter moon on its back and a galaxy of stars. We had a rough voyage but reached a sheltered anchorage and comparative calm at around midnight. When we saw at first morning light how close inshore he had safely brought his ship and navigated it among so many jagged rocks, we praised our Captain for his skill and courage.

If one could visit but a single island in the Galapagos Archipelago, it would be Hood. As we approached it after battling for six hours against a heavy swell and at a distance of some ten sea miles from shore we were met by a pair of dolphins which sported around the ship with incredible speed. Surely this must be one of the most graceful of all God's greatures? They swam side by side in perfect unison, now leaping out of the water together like well trained circus horses, now crossing underneath our keel, now racing ahead with such acceleration as to make our boat seem stationary. They had such grace and harmony of movement that it was a pleasure to watch them and they gave the impression of giving this wonderful exhibition of strength and skill for the sheer joy of it.

Nearer to land sea-lions were continually popping their heads out of the water to take a good look at us to try to satisfy their insatiable curiosity. Then we saw Pelicans flying in long lines on some well planned fishing trip, and Boobies diving vertically from a great height as do all the Gannet family. The front of their skulls is thickened to withstand the terrific impact as they hit the water and this I have seen from examining the skulls of dead Gannets. I have heard it said that many lose their sight from the same cause, but this I have only on hearsay.

We made our landfall at Punta Suarez but the waves were breaking on the rocks with great force. Pedro said he had never seen it so rough at Hood. But we knew we would want every minute of the two days we had allotted to this wonderful island and so he anchored well off shore and we piled into the dinghy with our sailor and were swept through the breakers into a sheltered cove as if it had been the lagoon of a coral island.

The first sight to greet our wondering eyes was the colony of Blue-footed Boobies now nesting – by far the biggest colony of this species in the islands. They were just starting their breeding; most were coupled and had staked out their territories but only one was brooding its single egg. They are quaint birds, like Gannets black and white but with vivid pale blue legs and feet, of which they appear to be inordinately proud. As one partner returned to another they both performed the greeting ceremony. They were quite unafraid of us as we walked amongst them filming but the male would hiss and whistle at any one of us whose footsteps trespassed on his territory and the female uttered a harsh squawk. These birds are not endemic to Hood but are found on most of the islands and along the west coast of South America but breed only on Hood and Daphne. They lay two or three eggs and so were at an early stage of breeding and seemed more interested in definition of territory.

There is also on Hood a much smaller breeding colony of the Masked Booby, of which the white head has a black 'mask' and legs are flesh coloured. They were more advanced in breeding; we saw several chicks of eight weeks or so.

The most tremendous sight on Hood is the breeding colony of the Waved Albatross. This is alleged to be unique. From their lonely wanderings over the vast expanse of the southern oceans of the world, they gather to breed along the cliff tops of Hood at about six metre intervals. A scrape in the ground serves them as a nest in which to incubate the single white egg. Their courtship display is the fencing and clattering of the two giant yellow bills; it is a greeting and a strengthening of the pair bond created in earlier years after an absence of ten months and is not concerned with selection of a partner or the prelude to mating. These long-living birds do not breed until five years old and then appear to pair for life. They are silent birds and their cry during this greeting ceremony is never heard at other times. It has been likened to the braying of an ass.

Each parent takes its turn at incubation which may last for several days, during which the sitting bird neither eats nor drinks. When the single chick is finally hatched, it is fed by both parents with oil excreted from their stomachs. On being relieved of its sitting duty the Albatross raises itself majestically from the nest and walks awkwardly on its weak legs and three-toed webbed feet to the edge of the cliff whence it launches itself into the air. Despite its incredibly low weight to wing-area ratio, it cannot take flight from level ground. Its weight is eight to nine pounds but its eight foot wing span, which is so efficient in soaring over the ocean surface, is a real handicap in becoming airborne. These huge and solemn birds were quite unperturbed by our presence amongst them. They paid us scant attention, presumably being entirely pre-occupied by the important business of hatching and rearing their single offspring to secure continuance of their highly specialised race.

We remained at anchor in Punta Suarez that night and early in the morning the cruise ship *Floriana* came in and presently put a few passengers ashore, where they were guided to see the Albatross breeding colony. But their visit was brief for they were soon on board again and the ship left at 11.00 a.m. I do not doubt that much of their visit was spent in watching the spectacular water spout caused by the Pacific rollers surging into an underground tunnel and then bursting through a blow-hole in its roof under great pressure to a height of at least thirty metres with an accompanying roar.

The National Park yacht came in to land a consignment of young tortoises with their carapaces all indelibly numbered for later checking. They wasted no time in completing their task and left before we could talk with them. We filmed the Red-billed Tropic Birds flying directly from sea to their breeding sites scattered along the face of tall and inaccessible cliffs. But they fly so fast with their long white tail feathers streaming out behind them that the footage we shot of them was unsatisfactory. We turned our attention to make some good pictures of the picturesque Swallow-tailed Gull. This must surely be the loveliest of all gulls. Besides being the most colourful, it is the only gull in the world to be partially nocturnal. It is a symphony in soft grey and white with a bright crimson eye-ring and red legs and feet. It is very plentiful around all the islands and makes a scrape among the pebbles to lay and incubate its single speckled egg. It breeds at any time of year at intervals of nine to ten months, in consequence of which the young and immature, very different in plumage, may be seen at all stages of development.

There is only one other gull breeding in the Archipelago, the Lava Gull, which is rather odd on these oceanic islands when different species of gull will follow a ship so far. This is also named the Dusky Gull; it is less numerous than the Swallow-tailed and no more than 400 pairs are believed to have survived. It is found nowhere else in the world and hopefully its protection will avoid this being yet another extinct species. It is not a very attractive bird either in appearance or habits. Its plumage is a uniform dull grey and in feeding it is both a predator and a scavenger. It picks up much of its food along the tideline but will also scavenge around stationary boats and the few buildings of habitation. It will steal the eggs and young nestlings of other sea birds left momentarily unprotected and will eat the very young marine iguanas.

Hood Mocking Birds

The Galapagos Dove is another species unique to these islands and widespread throughout them, being a sufficiently strong flier to colonise them all where the food supply of seeds is adequate. Unhappily it is now extinct on islands where feral cats, introduced by man, have totally destroyed the race. This is sad because it is the only representative of that vast and world-wide family, the Columbidae, which embraces all the doves and pigeons. And it is one of the most colourful of a beautiful family, having a soft grey plumage and a vivid blue eye-ring. It falls an easy prey to cats, being a most trustful bird which shows no fear of man unless one approaches very close to the hen sitting on her two white eggs in the untidy nest of dried grass scarcely concealed amongst the rocks, when it will slip off the nest and feign injury by the usual broken wing trick.

In the afternoon of our second day on Hood we filmed some of the finches, and the Hood Mocking Bird. This is a distinct species from the Galapagos Mocking Bird, though similar in appearance, having evolved separately on this remote island as it has also done on Charles and Chatham islands, developing over millenia sufficient anatomical differences to qualify for specific identification.

There are many colourful and harmless lizards – geckoes, basilisk, and lava species. Their movements are as swift as elsewhere and difficult to photograph. We found a lava lizard making a meal of a large spider which kept it in one place long enough to expose some footage of film on it. They help to control the abundant insect life and in turn provide a food supply for the Galapagos Hawk and the other carnivorous predators, the Barn Owl and the Short-eared Owl. Before the arrival of man the flora and fauna must have achieved a perfect balance. But the introduction by man of exotic species and pests upset this Garden of Eden ecosystem; the collection of specimens of rare endemic species for the museums of the world added a new threat in the last century and the early decades of this. And now the developing pressures of human visitors presents a fresh problem for those who are trying to preserve this scientific treasure house for posterity.

We sailed throughout the night to reach the island of South Plaza at 09.00 hours helped by a strong favourable current. We anchored in calm water between North and South Plaza, which lie close together and not far off Santa Cruz. The nearest point of that island is a great red rock only about one and a half kilometres distant, known as 'Look Out Point', which again is traditionally the vantage point from which pirates kept a look-out for more legitimate vessels to plunder or to avoid.

We went ashore on South Plaza at 09.30 and here we immediately found plenty of land iguanas. These reptiles are smaller than the one we saw at Conway Bay – about a metre long and of a more yellow hue. They have a row of spines along the back. They are relatively tame and do not immediately rush to their burrows on encounter. They are very partial to bananas and their tolerance of humans is due to being fed these fruits by visitors.

This abundance of land iguanas on South Plaza is artificial. Their traditional breeding areas of Conway Bay and on Isabella were invaded by dogs introduced by man and allowed to run wild to the extent that the slaughter proved disastrous. Eighty-five survivors were collected and released on South Plaza where they have lived safely but do not appear to have increased in number. Little is known about the social system or the reproductive process of this unique lizard, which is unlike that of any known genus. Attempts may now be made to breed them in captivity.

South Plaza is devoid of fresh water and the iguanas evidently obtain all the liquid they need from their vegetarian diet, which includes the fruit of the prickly pear cactus. They spend most of their day in shallow burrows which appears to be an avoidance of a rise in temperature by exposure to the sun. This is directly contrary to the habit of the marine iguana which seeks all the direct rays of the sun to raise its temperature.

The formalised battles between male land iguanas defending their territories has aroused great interest and we were fortunate to witness and film one of them. They meet head on and seize some portion of each other's tough and leathery hide in their powerful jaws. Then follows a protracted pushing and pulling and manoeuvring for position until eventually one – usually the interloper – recognises defeat and turns tail. Throughout the engagement there is no attempt on the part of either combatant to inflict any real injury on the opponent, which could readily be done with their powerful jaws and rows of teeth top and bottom. It is as if preservation of the race was recognised as being of more importance than individual victory and so they fight according to strict rules of combat like knights at a joust.

South Plaza is a small island like a table tilted at about thirty degrees up towards the south. It is covered with the sessuvium bush which was green but already beginning to turn red as it is for most of the year. On top of the sheer cliff some forty metres high we had an excellent view of the constant procession of sea birds at the same level or beneath us – Frigates, Pelicans, Gulls, Tropic Birds, and Shearwaters – beautiful to watch but difficult to film satisfactorily. In particular we studied the ungainly tumble into the water of the Pelican, contrasting with the arrow dive of the Boobies.

Sea-lions were here more plentiful and tamer than anywhere we had watched them. To satisfy their curiosity they would clamber into our dinghy when moored to the small wood jetty; and I found I could pat them on the head like a dog. But some adults sleeping on the jetty resented being moved or stepped over and turned quite aggressive when shifted out of the way.

A Cactus Finch was constructing a nest between two fleshy spikes of an opuntia cactus; I tried to film it at work but it would not come in whilst I watched. The nest was woven of dry grass with a domed roof and a side entrance.

On the following morning at 04.30 hours we sailed north to visit the uninhabited island named Daphne, and reached it at 08.30. This is the top of an extinct volcano with nearly sheer sides and a wide crater at the summit. There is no sheltered inlet and no anchorage as the mountain sides drop sheer to sixty fathoms so we scrambled ashore from the dinghy which returned to our boat and it kept station as best it could to return to pick us up when we signalled.

The attraction of Daphne is the huge breeding site of Boobies.

On the floor of the crater, some 300 metres below the rim, there are hundreds of nests of the Blue-footed Booby and on the outer slopes a lesser number of nests of the Masked Booby. I had a request from Mr Mike Harris to report the breeding stage of the Blue-footed and to count the number of breeding pairs, which I did and reported to him on our return about 400 pairs. To look into this crater was a truly fantastic sight for it simulated a refugee camp in which these oceanic birds had gathered from far reaches of the Pacific to this secluded and safe place annually to rear the next generation. Adult birds coming and going with fish, young ones at various stages leaving the nest, and some parents still sitting. A few well developed youngsters were standing on rocks to perform their wing-exercising preparatory to trying a flight. We watched fascinated for all the time we could spare. There were many Red-billed Tropic Birds flying to and fro but we had no time to locate their breeding place.

We were not left marooned on Daphne but were taken thence to Barero Bay on the northern coast of Santa Cruz where the lagoon is extensive and is entered through a mangrove swamp. These are stilt mangroves and the lagoon level was unusually low so that we had to haul the dinghy through shallow water by pulling on the mangrove roots. We were accompanied on this journey into the lagoon by mantas which swim like butterflies. These were not the giant manta but measured about one and a half metres across the 'wings'. Within the lagoon green turtles were swimming on the surface steadily and without concern for us, having some destination clearly in mind.

A flock of Yellow Warblers bathing in the shallow water on the tide line made a pretty picture to use up the last few feet of film that remained. And having shot it all, we were tantalised by having none to record the antics of a Lava Heron which was perched precariously on a branch low over the water trying to seize flies on the surface by sudden elongations of its neck and stabs of its dagger bill. High above us we spotted the familiar silhouette of an Osprey. These lovely birds of prey are scattered world-wide in tropic and temperate regions wherever freshwater lakes provide an ample food source. They are well equipped to plummet into the water to lift a fish from its element and grip it in specially adapted talons.

We sailed gently to nearby Baltra island on which lies the only airstrip. We had no guarantee of three seats in the plane due to fly back to Guayaquil the following day but we kept hoping. Our short-wave radio had repeatedly told us that one seat would be available but not three. And each of us had urgent and different reasons to reach home.

In the tiny port of Baltra we moored alongside a yacht on which were two U.S.A. youngsters who had been on a Greenpeace or similar mission – a boy and a girl. They were due to fly to the mainland on the following day and they had confirmed seats on the plane. Obviously they found each other's company congenial. They told us that they would dearly like to stay in the Galapagos for another week but their yacht had to be returned for another charter tomorrow and they had no money to charter a boat. Captain Pedro told us he had no charter for his boat and was free to take them. We told them that we had some money left but were short of time. So we did a deal – their two plane seats for our payment of a week's charter and all parties were satisfied.

We drew their attention to a brass plate fixed above the stairway leading from the deck of the cabin of our boat. In translation it read – 'Marriages solemnised by the Captain on this boat are valid for the duration of one voyage only'.

We handed over our quarters to the starry-eyed couple and said farewell to our excellent Captain, guide, and crew.

Index of Bird Names